SOUL KEEPING

"Soul keeping is simply growing in loving relationship with Jesus Christ. This book beckons us from the shallowness of modern life to time-honored paths of soul keeping practiced by prophets, psalmists, Jesus, disciples, martyrs, and saints. Howard Baker shows us that soul keeping is really about soul losing—relinquishing one's soul into the arms of Jesus. Here is a fine contribution to the literature of Christian spirituality."

> —DR. BRUCE DEMAREST, professor of theology and spiritual formation, Denver Seminary

"I went to college and seminary with Howard Baker, during which time we worked together in ministry. I love and respect him and count it an honor to be numbered among his friends. It is both a joy and a privilege to recommend his first book *Soul Keeping*."

> —KEN GIRE, author of *Moments with the Savior* and *Windows of the Soul*

"Many evangelicals have come to me seeking guidance for intimate and heartfelt relationship with Jesus. With the publication of *Soul Keeping*, I will simply recommend this remarkable book."

> —BRENNAN MANNING, author of *Abba's Child* (NavPress)

SOUL KEEPING

ANCIENT PATHS OF SPIRITUAL DIRECTION

BY

HOWARD BAKER

NAVPRESS®

BRINGING TRUTH TO LIFE

OUR GUARANTEE TO YOU

We believe so strongly in the message of our books that we are making this quality guarantee to you. If for any reason you are disappointed with the content of this book, return the title page to us with your name and address and we will refund to you the list price of the book. To help us serve you better, please briefly describe why you were disappointed. Mail your refund request to: NavPress, P.O. Box 35002, Colorado Springs, CO 80935.

The Navigators is an international Christian organization. Our mission is to reach, disciple, and equip people to know Christ and to make Him known through successive generations. We envision multitudes of diverse people in the United States and every other nation who have a passionate love for Christ, live a lifestyle of sharing Christ's love, and multiply spiritual laborers among those without Christ.

NAVPRESS, BRINGING TRUTH TO LIFE, and the NAVPRESS logo are registered trademarks of NavPress. Absence of ® in connection with marks of NavPress or other parties does not indicate an absence of registration of those marks.

NavPress is the publishing ministry of The Navigators. NavPress publications help believers learn biblical truth and apply what they learn to their lives and ministries. Our mission is to stimulate spiritual formation among our readers.

Library of Congress Catalog Card Number: 98-28275
ISBN 1-57683-049-7

Photo illustration by Steve Eames

Some of the anecdotal illustrations in this book are true to life and are included with the permission of the persons involved. All other illustrations are composites of real situations, and any resemblance to people living or dead is coincidental.

Unless otherwise identified, all Scripture quotations in this publication are taken from the *New American Standard Bible* (NASB), © The Lockman Foundation 1960, 1962, 1963, 1968, 1971, 1972, 1973, 1975, 1977. Other versions used include: the *HOLY BIBLE: NEW INTERNATIONAL VERSION* ® (NIV®). Copyright © 1973, 1978, 1984 by International Bible Society. Used by permission of Zondervan Publishing House. All rights reserved. *The Message: New Testament with Psalms and Proverbs* (MSG) by Eugene H. Peterson, copyright © 1993, 1994, 1995, used by permission of NavPress Publishing Group; and the *King James Version* (KJV).

Baker, Howard, 1951-
   Soul Keeping : ancient paths of spiritual direction / by Howard Baker.
        p. cm.
   ISBN 1-57683-049-7 (pbk.)
   1. Spiritual direction.   I. Title
   BV5053.B34   1998
   253.5'3—dc21   98-28275
                                                                                        CIP

Printed in the United States of America

3 4 5 6 7 8 9 10 11 12 13 14 15 16 / 14 13 12 11 10 09 08 07 06 05

For Janis

Lifelong companion on these paths—
Always at my side,
Often several steps ahead.
Her love and prayers draw me—
Onward, Inward, Upward.

CONTENTS

PART ONE:
Invitation to Soul Keeping

PART TWO:
The Ancient Paths

ACKNOWLEDGMENTS

David Hazard . . . Thank you for your gracious, encouraging, and skillful work as editor to a first-time author. Through the process you have become my friend, and I your apprentice in the craft of writing.

The staff of Young Life in the Rocky Mountain Region—especially Bill Maston . . . Thank you for providing me community—the soil out of which this book grew.

The students of Denver Seminary, of Fuller Seminary Colorado, and of the Formation Program for Spiritual Directors . . . Thank you for deepening this material by your questions, affirmations, and interactions.

Those who have led me on these paths . . . Thank you Brennan Manning, Eugene Peterson, Vie Thorgren, and Bruce Demarest, for not only teaching me, but showing me the life of soul keeping.

Lynda Graybeal and Richard Foster . . . Thank you for referring the wonderful people at NavPress to me, resulting in the invitation to write this book.

Janis, Keely, and Cody . . . Thank you for being the face of Christ to me every day. Without the love, joy, and inspiration you bring into my life, I would have never picked up the pen to write.

GENERAL INTRODUCTION

by Dallas Willard

The SPIRITUAL FORMATION LINE presents discipleship to Jesus Christ as the greatest opportunity individual human beings have in life and the only hope corporate mankind has of solving its insurmountable problems.

It affirms the unity of the present-day Christian with those who walked beside Jesus during His incarnation. To be His disciple then was to be with Him, to learn to be like Him. It was to be His student or apprentice in kingdom living. His disciples heard what He said and observed what He did. Then, under His direction, they simply began to say and do the same things. They did so imperfectly but progressively. As He taught: "Everyone who is fully trained will be like his teacher" (Luke 6:40).

Today it is the same, except now it is the resurrected Lord who walks throughout the world. He invites us to place our confidence in Him. Those who rely on Him believe that He knows how to live and will pour His life into us as we "take His yoke . . . and learn from Him, for He is gentle and humble in heart" (Matthew 11:29, emphasis added). To take His yoke means joining Him in His work, making our work His work. To trust Him is to understand that total immersion in what He is doing with our life is the best thing that could ever happen to us.

To "learn from Him" in this total-life immersion is how we "seek first his kingdom and his righteousness" (Matthew 6:33). The outcome is that we increasingly are able to do all things, speaking or acting as if Christ were doing them (Colossians 3:17). As apprentices of Christ we are not learning how to do some special religious activity, but how to live every moment of our lives from the reality of God's kingdom. I am learning how to live my actual life as Jesus would if He were me.

If I am a plumber, clerk, bank manager, homemaker, elected official, senior citizen, or migrant worker, I am in "full-time" Christian sevice no less than someone who earns his or her living in a specifically religious role. Jesus stands beside me and teaches me in all I do to live in God's world. He shows me how, in every circumstance, to reside in His Word and thus be a genuine apprentice of His—His disciple indeed. This enables me to find the reality of God's world everywhere I may be, and thereby to escape from enslavement to sin and evil (John 8:31-32). We become able to do what we know to be good and right, even when it is humanly impossible. Our lives and words become constant testimony of the reality of God.

A plumber facing a difficult plumbing job must know how to integrate it into the kingdom of God as much as someone attempting to win another to Christ or preparing a lesson for a congregation. Until we are clear on this, we will have missed Jesus' connection between life and God and will automatically exclude most of our everyday lives from the domain of faith and discipleship. Jesus lived most of His life on earth as a blue-collar worker, someone we might describe today as an "independent contractor." In His vocation He practiced everything He later taught about life in the kingdom.

The "words" of Jesus I primarily reside in are those recorded in the New Testament Gospels. In His presence, I learn the goodness of His instructions and how to carry them out. It is not a matter of meriting life from above, but of receiving that life concretely in my circumstances. Grace, we must learn, is opposed to earning, not to effort.

For example, I move away from using derogatory language against others, calling them twits, jerks, or idiots (Matthew 5:22), and increasingly mesh with the respect and endearment for persons that naturally flows from God's way. This in turn transforms all of my dealings with others into tenderness and makes the usual coldness and brutality of human relations, which lays a natural foundation for abuse and murder, simply unthinkable.

Of course, the "learning of Him" is meant to occur in the context of His people. They are the ones He commissioned to make disciples, surround them in the reality of the triune name, and teach them to do "everything I have commanded you" (Matthew 28:20). But the disciples we make are His disciples, never ours. We are His apprentices along with them. If we are a little farther along the way, we can only echo the apostle Paul: "Follow my example, as I follow the example of Christ" (1 Corinthians 11:1).

It is a primary task of Christian ministry today, and of those who write for this line of books, to reestablish Christ as a living teacher in the midst of His people. He has been removed by various historical developments:

assigned the role of mere sacrifice for sin or social prophet and martyr. But where there is no teacher, there can be no students or disciples.

If we cannot be His students, we have no way to learn to exist always and everywhere within the riches and power of His Word. We can only flounder along as if we were on our own so far as the actual details of our lives are concerned. That is where multitudes of well-meaning believers find themselves today. But it is not the intent of Him who says, "Come to me . . . and you will find rest for your souls" (Matthew 11:28-29).

Each book in this line is designed to contribute to this renewed vision of Christian spiritual formation and to illuminate what apprenticeship to Jesus Christ means within all the specific dimensions of human existence. The mission of these books is to form the whole person so that the nature of Christ becomes the natural expression of our souls, bodies, and spirits throughout our daily lives.

INTRODUCTION

By David Hazard

Following pathways is an essential part of our lives. I am speaking of the healthy routines and patterns we establish to bring order to our days and lead us step by step to our various life goals.

The salesman organizes his week of appointments; the CEO sets her quarterly and annual goals; the student—of martial arts, or the cello, or business administration—follows a path of study to take hold of the skill she seeks; the wise parent helps his children explore colleges and careers—helping them to find a career path that's a right "fit," and satisfying.

Only in our spirituality have we balked at the concept of following a set "path"—a certain discipline of prayer, study, or commitment to any kind of daily pattern.

Perhaps we have been too influenced by western, humanistic (and romantic) ideas that the soul should be left alone to "soar," to "wander," to "find its own path." We have held up the ideal of "the individual," while forgetting that, on his own, the individual is more often lost and confused and needing guidance than "enlightened," or "whole," or free enough of neuroses and outer pressures to choose his own path.

Perhaps we carry prejudices against the older branches of the Church. So we mistakenly throw out healthy spiritual practices with "the bathwater" of doctrines and a church government we don't like.

And so we find ourselves and other Christians struggling to stay true to Christ and pushed off course by interior winds of depression, boredom, dryness, or apathy. We have a very tough time staying in the "spiritual race" that Paul described. Who will help us keep our soul on track; keep us growing deeper and stronger in the living Spirit of Christ; keep us out of "sloughs of despond" and pressing through in godly living when we are plain bored at the core of our being?

Howard Baker has written *Soul Keeping* to introduce you to a number of the time-honored "spiritual paths" practiced by masters of

Christian spirituality. With so much written about the soul and spiritual disciplines today, the author makes it plain that he is writing to the disciple of Jesus Christ—the man or woman who wants both to grow in Christian character and find tried and true paths that will keep him or her on a healthy inward track to spiritual peace and freedom when so much in life tries to push believers off course and leave us bogged in our emotions. *Soul Keeping* will help you find the "path" to a deeper experience of Christ and help you move beyond emotions that are limiting your growth in maturity. And so we are pleased to make this work a part of our Spiritual Formation Line.

DAVID HAZARD

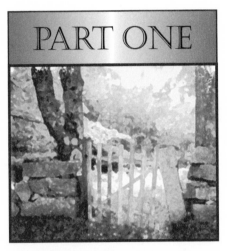

PART ONE

INVITATION TO SOUL KEEPING

CHAPTER ONE

KEEPING THE SOUL

". . . ask for the ancient paths, *where the good way is and walk in it; and you shall find rest for your souls. . . ."*

JEREMIAH 6:16

The most terrifying moment of my life was realizing that I had lost my five-year-old daughter Keely in a crowd of 100,000 people at a Mayfest celebration in Ft. Worth some fifteen years ago. The memory of that event chills me to this day. We were walking along with another dad and daughter when she wandered off, innocently and inconspicuously. Within an hour, we found her. A volunteer had taken her by the hand and led her safely to the spot where we were reunited. I was spared the capital punishment that my wife would have pronounced as sentence for my crime.

The lessons that have stayed with me from that experience are these: First, my child needs a competent companion who will keep his eye on her. Second, she needs to stay close to that companion. Third, she needs to know that the way to stay close to her companion—in this case, me—is to hold my hand and keep her eyes on me at all times.

Like the spiritual children we are, you and I can experience times—even long periods—when we feel lost and confused, sensing that we have lost sight of our Father. In life's crowding events, it's as if He has walked away from us.

God is always leading us somewhere. Do we understand this? Most often, we are focused on our own goals and plans, and before we know it, we feel as if we are on our own. We look up and realize that we have no idea where God is in our lives. We sense a separation from God, even though a firm knowledge of Scripture tells us He is "very near."

For many good people of faith, God can seem impossibly far away—somewhere beyond the fog of boredom, anxiety, depression, and despair that is all we seem to see ahead. How did we come to feel this directionless?

Today, many Christians are finding that they need the help of older Christians and "mentoring" from the classic, directive writings of past spiritual masters. What they sense is a need for soul care—that is, a need to keep their souls directed in a healthy growth that (1) allows them to understand God's constant presence and work in their lives and (2) helps them make sense of chaotic interior conditions—like periods of enthusiasm followed by sheer boredom and restlessness—that dot their spiritual path like confusing patches of sunlight and shade.

Many of us have recognized the need to have others who understand the working and ways of God and the human soul to guide us. What we have recognized is a need for what I call "soul keeping"—that is, the need to be helped along on a healthy path of Christian spiritual growth when we feel stale or stuck.

WANDERING

As Christians, we encourage growth in service, growth in scriptural knowledge, and growth in commitment to marriage, family, and church. Why have we nearly ignored the soul's growth? Before we can sort out our confusion or stagnation, we need to understand the soul itself.

Scripture gives us a wonderful image that describes the soul of humankind: "All of us like sheep have gone astray" (Isaiah 53:6). Many of us have understood this as referring to our spiritual state before conversion, when our pursuit of sin kept us separated from God. But I also believe, from my years as a Christian and my work as a spiritual director for others, that it also accurately depicts our ongoing tendency to lose sight of God and wander off from Him. We then find ourselves in trackless places of the soul, where things are dry and little makes sense.

If we are honest, most of us would admit that our ability to sense and stay close to God is still relatively immature. How often do we sense that we are cut off, in one way or another, from the ability to hear God and know His guiding hand on our lives? And why is it so hard for some of us to admit that we have lived with this disconnected-from-God feeling for too long?

Is it that we are afraid to be honest? Perhaps we're afraid to admit the true condition of our soul because we are afraid to discredit scriptural truths about God's constant love and invisible presence. Perhaps we have been taught that "faith is accepting God's Word as fact, *whether or not we feel anything.*" Yes, God's Word is true, no matter what emotions tell us. And yes, it is a bumpy ride through life if we always give in to our emotional states, which can change like the wind.

But there is a danger in ignoring our interior state. For as sensations from our physical nerve endings alert us to outer conditions, so the state of our soul often tells us we need to locate and pay attention to God again, so we can understand how He is guiding our lives. Ignoring what our soul is trying to tell us leads to spiritual atrophy, the way ignoring pain in a muscle can cause long-term tissue damage.

What are we to do if we lose the sense of God's nearness, leadership, and care? What if we find ourselves living too long in fields of sadness, restlessness, doubt, or dryness?

DIRECTION FOR THE WANDERING SOUL

The word *pastor* describes a "shepherd of souls"—someone competent in the art and practice of guiding us safely back to the greater care of God. One job of a pastor is to meet us where we are, in our various states of confusion and separation, and "keep" us—in the sense of tending a soul. This is also the job of those in the body of Christ known as *spiritual directors.* To direct a soul does not mean to take over responsibility for someone else's growth. It means to locate the places where someone is stuck in spirit and to redirect his steps. The goal is not mere emotional comfort or healing, though that is important, too. The goal is to reunite the individual with a clear sense of God's presence, work, care, and direction—what the apostle Paul calls a "ministry of reconciliation" between the believer and God (2 Corinthians 5:18). This is the work of "soul keeping," as it is practiced by spiritual men and women who know how to direct the soul in its growth in Christ.

Someone who is a trained pastor or spiritual director can help those who are lost or foundering, in the same way that a competent adult found my straying daughter and led her back to me. But it is also possible for each of us, as everyday Christians, to learn something of the art and practice of soul keeping. Pastors and spiritual directors are not omnipresent or omniscient, and they will not always be aware when life throws us off course or when we seem to be off the path and in a desert or wilderness place.

Before we go further, I also want to be sure you are clear about the "path" to which I am referring because there are many "paths" being offered to us today. I am referring to spiritual growth in the character of Jesus Christ. That means not only spiritual comfort and basic instruction, but a change in the attitudes of the inner man, the inclinations of our heart, so that a man or woman grows in the passion to pursue God and live life more fully under His guidance and in His service. The ultimate goal of soul keeping is to move us beyond ourselves and our focus on personal interests so that we become people who are living life "in Christ," not merely in our own natural human spirit.

What does this mean? To be "in Christ" means to have our will and energies given to the service of God, whatever that means in our individual lives. I'm afraid that for many Christians today this translates into busy, outward activity. We are talking here about influencing the heart, from which all our outer actions proceed. When it comes to the inner man and the inner conditions we all face, to be "in Christ" means this: to press on in soul with confidence and reassurance that God is leading us and instructing us as we learn how to go through our present interior state to find Him and His purposes that lie beyond the emotional stalemates we would rather not face.

In this, Jesus Himself is our best example. For as the writer of Hebrews tells us, "Let us fix our eyes on Jesus, the author and perfecter of our faith, who for the joy set before him endured the cross, scorning its shame, and sat down at the right hand of the throne of God" (Hebrews 12:2, NIV). We know that fulfilling God's highest, best purpose meant Jesus had to face not only the terrible circumstance of the cross itself, but to bravely press through all the inner conditions of soul a human would encounter in His position. Isn't it our boredom, depression, doubt, and independent attitude that keep our soul from pressing on to follow God?

Ultimately, then, soul keeping is the art of persevering in spirit in order to find the glory of God revealed in us and through us, on the far side of our struggles. Whereas you and I want to shy away from the confusion, dryness, frustration, and questioning, I believe God wants us to *face* these interior states—in the light of His real presence and good purpose for us, and with the help of wise, supportive counsel. I believe God wants us to face our soul's conditions, not run from them.

Before we can learn how to help ourselves, we need the companionship of others who understand how soul keeping works. Yet not all Christian leaders are trained in this old and necessary art. Where will we find wise, patient soul keepers with the spiritual vision for such a task?

We need more than "comforters" who want to help us achieve "inner peace," or help us feel "excited" and "happy" about life again. Our culture is full of men and women who can massage our emotional troubles. What we need, as Christians, is men and women who can open our eyes to how God Himself uses conditions of the soul to shape us for His purposes.

FOLLOWING THE GREAT SHEPHERD...
WITH A GOOD PURPOSE

You and I can learn a good deal about keeping our souls moving and growing in Christ. Fortunately, the first responsibility for keeping our soul rests with God. David, who had amazing spiritual vision at times, saw Him as One who "will keep your soul" in all its ways (Psalm 121:7) and as One who "restores" the soul when it is spent and weak (Psalm 19:7; 23:3). And so it is God's initiative, the compelling urge of His voice, the inner empowerment to get up and go after Him again, that is the power of grace itself. But responding to God's voice, using the energy He has given me to keep in His path, is the work I must do.

Jesus said, "In your patience possess"—or keep, or shepherd—"ye your souls" (Luke 21:19, KJV). Our part in soul keeping is to learn what Paul meant when he instructed us to "keep in step" with God in spirit (Galatians 5:25, NIV). We can learn how to find direction for our inner man when we feel lost, or are wandering and confused. With God's help, we can take charge of these living souls and direct them into God's pathways.

The psalmist certainly understood his part in following God in spirit. He "composed and quieted" his soul (Psalm 131:2). He "humbled" his soul with fasting (Psalm 35:13), took charge of his soul by speaking to it before God (Psalm 62:5; 116:7), and questioned his soul's condition (Psalm 42:5,11; 43:5). He directed his soul to "bless the LORD" (Psalms 103:2,22; 104:1) and to "praise the LORD" (Psalm 146:1), and he lifted up his soul to God (Psalm 143:8). Jesus confirmed that through the empowerment of grace, we, like the psalmists, can direct our soul toward Him (Matthew 16:26).

Thomas Kelly, in his classic *A Testament of Devotion*, paints a picture of one who, in the manner of Christ, has possessed his soul and directed it godward.

> There is a way of life so hid with Christ in God that in the
> midst of the day's business one is inwardly lifting brief
> prayers, short [bursts] of praise, subdued whispers of adoration

and of tender love to the Beyond that is within. One can live in a well-nigh continuous state of unworded prayer, directed toward God, directed toward people and enterprises we have on our heart. There is no hurry about it at all; it is a life unspeakable and full of glory, an inner world of splendor within which we, unworthy, may live. Some of you know it and live in it; others of you may wistfully long for it; it can be yours. Now out from such a holy Center come the commissions of life. Our fellowship with God issues in world concern. We cannot keep the love of God to ourselves.[1]

Soul keeping does restore a sense of well-being—but when all is said and done, the restored soul is filled with renewed enthusiasm for the service of God and for helping others. In fact, the one who is on the path of steady growth knows he or she must take part in guiding others, or face stagnation, and even lose what has been gained.

From our own struggles, God intends to lead us into deeper life in Him. And beyond our personal need to find our own way in spirit, we are being trained so that we can later lead others who wish to grow in a strong, living faith. We can become people who have an answer for the hope that is in us (1 Peter 3:15), people who, because we have gained understanding and depth in spiritual matters, know the right words and the right way to direct others to God, no matter what confused condition we find them in (2 Timothy 2:15).

For Christians, our lifework beyond leading someone *to* Christ is to know how to lead someone to grow deeper *in* Christ. And that means learning to take every condition of soul, as well as every thought, "captive" (2 Corinthians 10:5). Like Jesus Himself, our high calling is to be conformed to the purposes of God.

DIRECTORS OF THE SOUL

Earlier I asked, "Where will we find wise, patient soul keepers with the spiritual vision for the task?"

In our Christian past, spiritual men and women understood the ways of the soul and how to guide others into a deeper, closer experience with God. Like Jeremiah before them, they directed Christians to "ask for the ancient paths, where the good way is, and walk in it; and you shall find rest for your souls" (Jeremiah 6:16). The paths of the soul are "ancient" because they seem to be the oldest paths on which men and women have found God, pressing through their personal turmoil to seek *direct* knowledge of Him.

Abraham, pondering the glory of the stars, encountered the One who spoke with creating power from beyond the cold indifference of the visible universe. Job pressed his soul along the path of frustration at the injustice of life and was given a new vision of the vastness of God's ways. The apostle Paul pursued God through the experiences that nearly brought him to despair at the impossible task of founding the young church, and after that he was given profound understanding of God's glory and plan in forming a "body of Christ" to share in God's suffering for His lost children.

Throughout the centuries, great saints and spiritual directors—like Francis of Assisi and Teresa of Avila in the Middle Ages, and contemporaries like Henri Nouwen—also learned the secret of focusing the passion of their whole being by walking the narrow way of Jesus that leads to life (Matthew 7:14).

The trouble with trying to seek God completely on our own is that we can so easily sink back into complacency and self-deception. Learning to live "in Christ" is incredibly challenging work. We would rather turn to easy distractions. We would rather blame God when life does not go our way, or piously tell ourselves we'll let Him explain Himself when we get to heaven, but we are called to seek Him and find Him *now.*

Today, we are beginning to rediscover the value of accepting guidance from a spiritual director. Christians of the past recognized the need to have someone "coach" them along in spiritual growth. The one offering direction was not a "guru" who had supposedly achieved perfection and therefore stood above them. Nor were they privy to "mystical secrets" or given ability to hear special voices and see secret visions on another's behalf. Instead, the spiritual director was a companion who could walk right beside someone, able to give direction because he or she understood the way to go through the dilemma and have a closer relationship with God on the other side of it. The spiritual director kept God in sight when the person had lost sight of Him. Who else could give us spiritual direction *out* of where we are struggling, stuck, or lost but one who has been there before—one who has learned how to fix his or her heart on things above?

My Hope for You

I discovered this need for competent soul guides in my own life many years ago. The trouble was, I didn't know where to find them. All around me there were astute Bible teachers, dynamic preachers, passionate evangelists, and skilled ministry organizers—but no spiritual guides. Many were willing to discuss the generalities of the Christian life, but I found no one willing to talk about the particulars of my soul's condition. I needed someone who appreciated my uniqueness as a person made in the image of God and who could help me make sense of the life-path on which God had me. Was there anyone who could bring spiritual insight to my condition? What I was longing for, but couldn't name, was the centuries-old Christian tradition of "spiritual direction." I will tell more about my own discoveries later.

For now, let me say that my goal in this book is to introduce you to some of the paths and practices of spiritual direction. By pursuing the wisdom of the Church's great spiritual directors, I discovered how to open my soul to the restoring, reviving work of God, and what it means to grow healthy in Christ. (In the next chapter, I will introduce you to these paths.) I discovered how to guide my life in light of two authoritative texts—the canon of Scripture and the "canon" of our lives. For God is both the author of the Word and the One who has authored a life-course for you and me (see Psalm 139): One has *been* written (the Word); the other is *being* written (our lives) as we learn to cooperate with God, allowing Him to do His work in us.

God's Story and Your Story Can Become One

My ultimate hope is that, by following the spiritual pathways (and perhaps seeking a spiritual director for yourself), you will find your soul's life through a greater connection with the Person and presence of God.

And so, as you will see, the raw material for spiritual growth comes from the grit of our life and human experience. For the Spirit of God calls us through our families of origin, our personalities, our choices, and all of the conditions of soul we encounter—and from that He forms in us the image of Himself and His grace which He wants to express to our particular world. From the dust of our lives, the glory of God can shine. He melds the two together in a *drama of redemption*, and even the struggles and wounds of my past can become sources of incredible compassion for others.

As Paul says, we are God's workmanship (Ephesians 2:10); that is, our lives are His *poiema*—literally, His poem. A poem is an artful creation, a thing of beauty that requires care and time to produce. My prayer is that you will find God slowly pulling together all the "words" of your life to achieve just the right meter and rhyme. For His high purpose is that your life may give voice to some piece of His holy wisdom and insight desperately needed by others in this challenging world.

A NEW START

Right now you may be experiencing boredom, complacency, burnout. By walking the paths that will give you new spiritual direction, you can move out of the places where you feel stuck in soul. You can experience within yourself a new purpose and new life as you learn to reconnect with God.

Today, make the commitment to a fresh start in spirit. What lies ahead is the peace and purpose your soul has been hungering for. Let's begin this new phase of your journey now, with an honest look at where we tend to lose the life of the inner person and how to begin restoring the soul in Christ.

CHAPTER TWO

FINDING THE SOUL

[Jesus said,] "Are you tired? Worn out? Burned out on religion? Come to me. Get away with me and you'll recover your life. I'll show you how to take a real rest. Walk with me and work with me—watch how I do it. Learn the unforced rhythms of grace."

MATTHEW 11:28-30, MSG

. . . for out of all of our doings and cares, our hopes and fears, and loves, [my uncle] makes a little home where the Spirit of Christ can dwell, and where, united to God by prayer, our souls can live and expand.

GWENDOLEN GREENE[1]

Years ago, I read a sheet of instructions, supposedly a page out of the manual for Peace Corps volunteers who were headed to South America. The title was, "What to Do If Attacked by an Anaconda." The instructions were as follows:

1. If you are attacked by an anaconda, do not run. The snake is faster than you are.
2. Lie flat on the ground.
3. Put your arms tight at your sides and your legs tight against one another.
4. The snake will come and begin to nudge and climb over your body.
5. Do not panic.
6. After the snake has examined you, it will begin to swallow you from the feet end. Always from the feet end.
7. The snake will now begin to suck your legs into its body. You must lie perfectly still. This will take a long time.
8. When the snake has reached your knees, slowly and with as little movement as possible reach down, take your knife and very gently slide it into the side of the snake's mouth, between the edge of its mouth and your leg. Then suddenly rip upwards, severing the snake's head.
9. Be sure your knife is sharp.
10. Be sure you have your knife.

One day, I repeated the instructions to several friends, and even used them to open talks. People got a laugh out of them—especially the last two instructions: Be sure your knife is sharp. Be sure you have your knife.

I knew it was macabre humor. But even as I passed the joke around, something deadly and invisible was opening its jaws and inching my soul inside. One day, I woke up to a feeling of absolute deadness inside, with no clue what had happened to me. I felt a cold panic because I was without anything resembling a knife.

Waking Up Dead

What I woke up to was the cold reality of the state of my inner life.

Though I had been working hard and long in an organization with a good cause, I had felt frustration at the meager results. Did I say frustration? It had festered into raw anger. Almost every day, alone in the car on my commute, I carried on blistering conversations in the back of my mind.

Then there was my personal life. I resisted looking honestly at myself there. Wasn't I a solid family man, giving as much time to my wife and children as possible? Didn't I love them and feel warm affections for every one of them? Somehow a voice inside kept booming, *Get real, Howard. Tell the truth.*

Alone, with my head in my hands, I admitted something I'd never told anyone before. Not even myself. I really, really did not want my wife or children to get too close because I didn't want them to meet the real me. I was intimidated by close, honest relationships. So my way of handling these people whom I insisted that I loved was to keep our relationships shallow, protecting myself.

I also woke up to the fact that my well-ordered outer life, with its busy, productive-looking schedule, was a disguise—not much more than an attempt to be in tight-fisted control of my inner world. If someone needed to get close for emotional or spiritual support, I was threatened. And then I'd withdraw into my own private realm—reading, playing sports, anything to keep from having to figure out how to deal with pieces of life I'd never mastered before.

So here I was, a Christian man, a guy working in Christian service, faced with a growing deadness inside. I was most of the way into the anaconda and joking about it.

For a long time, I was stuck in self-blame and self-pity. How could I let this happen to me? It was my job to be a "spiritual leader"; why had I let the spiritual passion go out of me? Then I'd wonder, how could God let this happen to me? After all, I was doing all the right things. I had biblical ethics and a "successful" ministry. I had the right theology, as far as I knew, so it wasn't that my Christian doctrine was flawed. But impeccable ethics and flawless theology were not enough.

LOSING MY WAY

Gradually, I came to see some basic missteps I'd made. Primarily, I had lost my soul to one of the chief rivals of devotion to Christ—that is, service for Him. As one writer put it, I had "dwarfed and narrowed [my] soul through a life of all work."[2] And I had convinced myself that the work was "for God." I did not even know how to develop a strong inner life. No one had ever told me how, and for me, it did not come naturally. So I was easy prey for the lurking anaconda that swallows souls.

About this time, I signed up for a retreat. I spent the first couple of days telling God what it was that He should do to straighten out my life. Soon I ran out of advice for God.

Then came my scheduled appointment with the retreat director.

The man immediately put me at ease by asking simple questions about my life. I told him about the years of ministry—long hours, dedication to people and a mission, a commitment to integrity and truth. He kept looking me in the eye warmly. I ventured a little deeper, opening up to him about the shallowness I felt. Then I came out with it. "I don't understand how I can be a Christian who is supposed to have God's Spirit living in me and be so empty." I felt a lump in my throat as I said it.

He studied me quietly. I didn't know what to expect. A reprimand? A spiritual "to do" list? I hoped not because I felt too tired and beaten for that.

"You have a strong belief system, a well-ordered moral life," he said in a moment. "And you work hard to serve others. You have everything . . ."

I looked at him and wanted to cry.

" . . . everything, Howard, but the fire."

My angry defenses went up. What was that supposed to mean? But inside I knew he was right.

He said more, directing me to look—openly, honestly before God— at my motives for what I was doing.

Honesty came harder than I thought. Until that moment I had not been desperate enough, or still long enough, to face the truth: I had to admit that I was really serving my own need to be successful and appreciated. The truth, so hard to face, was that I had lost the spiritual fire because my own ambitions had been the driving force in my life, rather than a love for God. Pride—that old, original, and hidden sin—had directed me away from serving God into serving an image of myself buried deep under layers of religious work.

Tough as this was to face, admitting the truth gave me the first glimmer of hope I'd had in a while. I felt an odd calm, a peace. I felt as if I was seeing my life somewhat from God's perspective. Just that much change—stepping out of my warped perspective and letting God's view form my thoughts—was enough to make me feel I might actually have a chance of starting again.

And so I discovered the benefits of allowing a spiritual director to take an honest look at my soul with me and direct me into the presence of God. I felt as if I might really be rejoining God on the path He had laid out for my life.

When I looked back, I felt sheepish at the superficial answers I'd had for deeper issues. At one point, in order to save my marriage, I'd had no choice but to cut back on my eighty-hour work weeks. Everyone had applauded my bold move and, secretly, honestly, that made me feel really good about myself. How shallow could I have been not to realize that the reason to save my marriage is my love for my spouse, not looking good in the eyes of others?

When I'd refused to face myself and my failings, I had turned to acceptable diversions such as sports, travel, hobbies, or friends. I'd also tried to fill in the emptiness with more prayer, more Bible study, more fellowship with other Christians, or more ministry—anything to avoid turning inward, to avoid asking the obvious questions: Why is this numbness here? What happened to my soul?

LOSING YOUR REAL SELF

In times past, people of faith sometimes posed this question to one another: "How is it with your soul?"

So . . . how *is* it with your soul? How full is your life with the sense of God's presence? Do you have a strong sense of His purposes for you, or is there a pit of boredom and emptiness, a sense that you are going through the motions of living? Are you disappointed in God, asking, "What good does it do to pray?" Are you drained by life's demands? If you were totally honest, would you have to admit you doubt that God cares about you? Do you wonder if He even exists?

When we fail to keep current with these deeply important issues of life, we allow our souls to be swallowed. We can tell ourselves it is "well" with our inner man because we believe the Bible and uphold right doctrine. But that does brutality to the living being inside each one of us, where we know the truth.

Some Christians have a difficult time with current talk about "spirituality" and understanding the "self." Shouldn't we stop focusing on ourselves and think only about serving God and others? Some have been taught that "the old self" needs to be "put to death," and we think that the first step in doing so is to ignore the inner person and its needs. Yet the soul cries out to us in our anxieties, furies, boredom, and confusion. Clearly, something inside needs to have our attention. Perhaps it is only when we have given a name to the need that we can make the crucial next step which turns spiritual growth into truly Christian spiritual growth. As we surrender our inner need to God for His care, we cooperate with His amazing work in us. And so, I believe we have a basic need to understand the true nature of the soul.

Soul occurs almost 300 times in our English Bibles, while the Greek word it comes from, *psyche*, actually occurs over 1,000 times.[3] This numerical discrepancy comes from the wide range of meanings that soul encompasses. Often the word psyche is rendered "life" or "self." We will define our use of soul as the most comprehensive term used in Scripture for the inner self which experiences the joys and sorrows of life and which relates to God.

A survey of the word soul tells us that our inner being is known by its conditions. The soul is disturbed, trembles, pines away, anguishes, is dismayed, sins, is troubled, despairs, is bitter, grieves, is tormented, loves, is poured out to God, is humbled, is restored, waits for the Lord, is redeemed, prospers, is healed, delights, sings praise, exults, rejoices, and, ultimately, takes refuge in God. Or, of course, it may try to find refuge in something else. In my case, the "refuge" was an image of myself as a minister. For others, refuge may be in possessions, another person, or an addiction.

In a word, my soul is the real me—the true me that I often keep hidden from the eyes of other people and even from myself. Sometimes I would like to hide this true self from the eyes of God.

What makes the soul such a powerful, life-directing influence is that its most elemental functions are longing, desiring, and yearning. When our inner longings are fulfilled, we experience joy, comfort, and peace—the inner bliss we mean when we say we have been blessed. When our longings are frustrated, we experience despair, trouble, and distress, among other unhappy states. All these conditions of the soul are normal and to be expected, even for mature people. This is why God's mission is to enter and come alive in the soul—and why we make a huge mistake when we ignore it. The soul holds the motivations that drive all we do.

Some of us understand "conversion" as a moment in time when we "turned to God," and yet what we need is the ongoing conversion of the inner person, which takes place continually as more and more of our motivating drive comes to light in His presence and comes under His governing direction.

In the past, Christians understood that God's goal was to gain the soul of man—to take up a position in the ground zero of our being. For this reason, God often works, or "moves upon us," to affect our interior conditions.

This is where learning to follow the paths of spiritual growth comes in. Many have found that these paths bring the soul into encounters with God and help us to see the motivations of our inner person in His light. Then we have a chance of turning from our old ways to pursue Him in an emerging new life.

When God moves upon the soul, affecting its conditions, we experience what has been called the actions of grace. For now, we will look briefly at each path we will cover later in the book.

The Path of Grace

Grace is what we encountered at salvation. We saw it in the death of Christ, offering Himself for our sins. We were moved by the action of God toward us, to draw us to Himself in the first place. But the graceful workings of God do not stop there.

The prophet Isaiah likened the spirit of humankind to the fragility of new spring grass, and he saw that it is God's breath moving across this sensitive soul within us that causes us to sense greater spiritual realities—such as our mortality and the fragility of life (Isaiah 40:6-8). We see that God has an active part in stirring the soul to wake us to spiritual needs. This is the ongoing aspect of grace — the truth about God's movement upon us and within us. It is something that we self-centered humans rarely take into account.

But we cannot ignore the possibilities of this grace because new growth opens up to us whenever we bring into the picture the possibility that God is at work. When I am bored, depressed, or confused, is God's Spirit moving upon me, trying to wake me to something, and calling me to seek Him in new, deeper ways? Is He trying to wean me from the false idols I attach myself to — say, my work, possessions, friends, shallow religion — so that I will seek my soul's life in Him?

The latest formula for successful Christian living will not meet the real need — that is, to recognize the movement and working of God, by which He remakes our inner person, heals our inner maladies, and empowers our growth into the fullness of Christ (Ephesians 4:13).

For fallen humans, however, learning to be truly open to God is the hardest lesson the soul must learn. Why? It is because, despite our first encounters with God's grace, an independent self-will lies buried in each of us. Pride is the "great interrupter" of spiritual growth. It is, as the ancients described it so vividly, "man turned in upon himself."

The Path of Humility

We need to be reintroduced to our Lord who was "meek"—whose power was in check — and also "humble in heart"—fully surrendered to God. We need to know more of Christ by walking with Him on the path of humility.

After we recognize the grace of God, humility is the basis for living "in Christ." Accepting our place in submission to God's greater purpose is among the most powerful moves we can make in spiritual maturity. This most basic Christlike attitude shows us how to move from self-centeredness to God-centeredness; from control to surrender; from busyness to rest under the direction of God through prayer and a growing awareness of God's imminent working in our everyday lives.

The Path of Wholehearted Prayer

To grow in spirit, we need to fully engage all that is within us with all we know of God — to wrestle with Him in prayer where need be, and to rest in Him in full trust where we are able. Some of us are good at pouring out our pain or doubt before God, but we're not so good at spending time dwelling on the transcendent visions of God that build our spiritual sight and our faith in Him. Others love to feel the soul-lift that praising God brings but are uncomfortable facing hidden pockets of anger, mistrust, or unwillingness to obey God.

We need a wholehearted prayer life so that we are growing in spiritual honesty and balance. This requires us to follow a path that will take us through the range of interior conditions that exists in every one of us. Fortunately, we have such a path.

The psalms rescue us from our fear of facing certain conditions of soul. They rescue us, too, from our fear of walking through interior confusion or discomfort. The psalms call to us, out of the depths of our human struggle, to connect with God. Praying the psalms gives us a well-rounded vocabulary with which to voice the soul's deepest cries. We can expect to find grace on this path because God inspired this prayer book for our sake, and it was the prayer book of Israel, of Jesus, and of the early church. We can move from superficial living into the depths of God's compassion, and here we meet God heart-to-heart, facing Him in our happiness and despondency, truthfulness and lying, integrity and hypocrisy.

The Path of Meditative Prayer

Some people love the thrill of finding good secondhand items at a garage sale or flea market. I am not one of them. For me there is nothing like lifting, say, brand-new shoes from the box. My senses delight in the supple, rich-smelling, authentic leather. It is the daily replenishment that comes with an authentic encounter with the God of all wonders that my soul craves as well. The work of opening my spiritual senses to God requires drive and originality, for because I am an individual, some of the ways I learn to open up to God must come from within me. Yet there is little encouragement today to seek God in new ways. The staleness of much of our twentieth-century spirituality testifies to this. Secondhand devotion cannot satisfy the desire for authentic encounter.

When we follow the path of meditative prayer—that is, meditating on Scripture—we open our soul in a way that can lead to a direct encounter with Jesus. Jesus' life and words become for us spirit and life, as if we are hearing them addressed to us personally. As we become immersed in a gospel story, for instance, our apathy and boredom can be injected by the powerful reality of a spirit-to-Spirit meeting with Jesus.

The Path of Silence and Solitude

Silence and solitude call us to quiet the demands and questions in our soul in order to allow God to fill us with answers, directions, graces, and gifts we could not possibly acquire by our own effort. Today we tend to believe that a full schedule will lead to a full soul. Yet the truth is, the busier we are, the more empty the soul becomes. I am not advocating "quietism" or "passivism"—there is a place for acting on our convictions—however, this age of information overload burns out the soul with its many empty words and messages. And what most of us desperately need is the restorative power of quietness and a lone encounter with our Maker.

In fact, when most of us try to get quiet, all we hear is the voice of our own anger, woundedness, resentment, greed, lust, doubt, and the like. Yet one of this century's greatest spiritual writers, Henri Nouwen, refers to solitude as God's "furnace of transformation."[4] It is in the quiet and solitary moment that we can learn to move through our wilderness of turmoil—to pass beyond our own perspectives—into the greater light of God's view of our circumstances and life. For those seeking God's voice in the chaos of living, silence and solitude form the path on which we learn to surrender our self, in the manner of Jesus, and discover a new fire of motivation coming from connecting with the greater will of the Father.

The Path of Spiritual Direction

Why is it that we are willing to go it alone on the spiritual journey in a day and age when we seek personalized assistance in almost every other facet of our lives?

Some of us believe we can create a "designer" Christianity, customized to fit our lifestyle and values. Others think we are meant to go it alone. But most of us wander on our own because we do not know where to go for help. Therefore we identify with the lament of the psalmist, "No one cares for my soul" (Psalm 142:4).

On the "path of spiritual direction" we uncover an all but forgotten discipline, one through which we can learn what God has for us as individuals who are also part of a divine scheme. The value of this path of spiritual direction is due to the fact that "there are no dittos among souls," as the great spiritual director von Hugel observed.[5] Each one of us is on a similar journey to Christlikeness and service to God, but it is not the same journey for everyone. We need a wise guide to point out the detours, identify the dead ends, and show us the smooth roads to travel on as we move out of a life that is centered in self and move into a life in which the purposes and compassion of God are coming alive in us.

HEART ON FIRE

When all is said and done, soul keeping brings all of us into the care and guidance of God—until we find ourselves living in the peaceful, eternal kingdom of God, more fully under His governing power than before. The apostle Paul gladly counted even the good things in his life as loss— literally, as manure—in comparison to the value of knowing Christ and keeping his soul for Him.

And so, soul keeping is not something we do merely for ourselves, even though we will realize personal benefits. It is something we do for God's sake, for the sake of becoming more intimately joined with Him and His life. The psalmists called this "thirsting for God." The passionate mystic John of the Cross expressed his "overwhelming desire" for God, saying, "I want to give myself completely to you. And I want you to give yourself completely to me."

In the words of A.W. Tozer, keeping the soul for God alone sums up the testimony of those he called "a grand army of fragrant saints":

> Come near to the holy men and women of the past and you
> will soon feel the heat of their desire after God. They mourned
> for Him, they prayed and wrestled and sought for Him day
> and night, in season and out, and when they had found Him
> the finding was all the sweeter for the long seeking.[6]

What would you give to feel your heart become on fire for living again? To feel the passion and meaning that come from being fully aware of God's presence?

Would you give attention to your own soul? Would you be willing to face the inner barriers, to seek God deeper and farther than you have sought Him before?

Along with Jesus and His many children of the burning heart, I invite you to turn from the formulas and shallow answers you may have been given, and to turn to the paths of the deeper spiritual life. What you have to gain is the beauty, passion, inner rest, and outward direction that describe the life of "abiding" in Christ (John 15). A renewed fire of the soul also comes from encountering the wondrous flame of God's love and life in you, from finding God Himself alive in you, as the strength of your being.

To begin, we will need to step back and take the long view. First, we must look at the struggle we all feel as our soul is pulled by incredible forces—either away from God or deeper into Him. Then we will look at the true journey of the soul, and how the Shepherd of our soul is already at work to lead us into deeper growth.

Following that, we will explore the classic paths of Christian spiritual growth—paths that will help restore our sense of spiritual direction as we move into a life that is more at one with God and His plan for us.

As many Christians have found, this is the way that will lead you beyond your self and into a renewed passion for living . . . finding your life in God.

CHAPTER THREE

BATTLE FOR THE SOUL

*"For what does it profit a man to gain the whole world,
and forfeit his soul?"*
MARK 8:36

*The great malady of the twentieth century, implicated
in all of our troubles and affecting us individually
and socially, is loss of soul.*
THOMAS MOORE[1]

None of her Christian friends would have imagined that Susan could walk out on her family and move in with another man. From the outside, everything looked ideal.

Susan's husband ran a successful insurance agency, and she was a loving mother to three adorable kids. But inside Susan was dying. In her hopes and dreams, she did not see herself locked into a world circumscribed by diaper changes and feeding and nap schedules. It seemed that all God, the church, and her husband wanted was for her to play the domestic role and be happy. And so a cold, silent despair had all but consumed Susan—when the other man came into her life.

Another person I know was losing himself in a less dramatic way. Carl had gone through the routines of a good life, slowly advancing in his career in computer technology, coaching his kids through the ranks of soccer teams, helping in the men's ministry at church. But on business trips the real Carl came out of hiding—the guy who drank too much and who indulged his fantasies in pornography. The hometown friends would have been shocked to see Carl on his latest business trip, getting so bold as to approach a pretty stranger in a bar and ask if she'd like to have dinner with him.

Now many of us would quickly condemn Susan and Carl for their drastic actions. Susan is confused and ashamed of what she's done and judges herself harshly. She experiences a desperate, sinking feeling that, in trying to solve some deep need, she has made the most terrible mistake of her life. Now she feels totally disconnected—from God, and even from herself. "Who am I? What kind of person would do this to her husband and her kids? What kind of person would betray everything she said she believed in?"

Many Christians would feel compelled to judge Susan's basic character. But as someone who has worked with desperate and failed

Christians, I am compelled to offer another answer: People can be so blindsided by unfilled needs they have ignored a sudden drive released from a reservoir within, practically catapulting them out of the "image" they have struggled to keep for years. When the soul is dying, even good people can do unexpected things.

Carl, too, condemns himself. For weeks after his trips, when the "nice guy" is back in town, the inner torture is brutal. How did he get to the point where he was, himself, two people inside one skin—a living lie?

In fact, Carl talked about his weaknesses several times years back, once with his pastor and another time with a ministry leader. The advice: Make a commitment to avoid evil and stick with it. He did not find a safe place to return to, to receive real attention for his soul's needs. What rings in the back of his mind are words from his pastor's sermon on men and commitment one Sunday: "A man who would cheat on his wife and family will experience the terrible anger of God. Because God ordained the family . . ."

So Carl lives in a "no man's land"—a zone where he is taught to "hate evil," and where there is no help offered for the temptations that are wound into his own flesh and blood. A zone where he feels like a Christian zombie, the living dead.

Both Susan and Carl are in a battle for their very souls. Who is helping them on the line of defense where they are weakest?

"THERE IS THEREFORE NOW TOO MUCH CONDEMNATION."

When we condemn and do not know how to help free people in spirit, we do a major disservice to the body of Christ—and to the other "soldiers" of God who are at war, as we are.

When we condemn other people, we betray the fact that a virulent force has infiltrated our ranks and is at work within us. It is the disease of judgmentalism—based on a flawed, limited ability to judge, at that. It is because most of us do not understand the depths of our own souls—much less anyone else's—that we are warned not to judge (see Matthew 7).

On the other hand, we are told to seek wisdom, or insight, and understanding about our inner person and our relationship to God and all things (see Proverbs 1). There were real needs in Susan—along with misconceptions, for sure—that weakened her inner resolve and drove her to sin against her family, herself, and ultimately against God.

It is sad to me that in both Susan's world and Carl's, all that was discussed were Christian ideals, while the reality of human struggle was given only the merest sign of recognition. Both felt judged and condemned for having the inner hungers at all, and that was the first defeat. Sometimes as Christians we do not acknowledge that our hungers are legitimate, even if the way we fantasize about fulfilling them is not.

It is doubly sad that when these two, and many other failed Christians, look for understanding from other believers — even pastors, to whom they look for soul care and healing — they often meet with still more judgment. The irony is this: When we judge people too quickly, without understanding the real needs of the soul that drive people to sin, then we leave ourselves open to attack and failure, too. In the end, our lack of insight about the life of the soul will lead us into trouble, and we wind up being judged, as well.

If we are going to win the struggle for the soul, we, as the body of Christ, must stop being so afraid to look at the motivating forces at work in us — or suddenly we will see more of our own begin living in dismal captivity to the very thing we are trying to avoid. This book is not focused on the matter of sin per se, or on overcoming temptation. But when we lose our sense of life within, we are far more likely to give in to something else that offers the false hope of restoring the inner fire we've been missing.

And so it is important to understand how we lose our soul, sometimes long before it is apparent to anyone else.

SOUL FOR SALE

Marilyn Monroe once quipped, "Hollywood's a place where they'll pay you a thousand dollars for a kiss and fifty cents for your soul."[2]

Sometimes it seems that we Christians will pay thousands of dollars to set up programs and crusades to "win" souls, but we give too little time to understanding, caring for, and growing Christian souls. We need to view the soul as it is viewed by the spiritual head of the Church, Jesus.

Jesus understood the depreciation in the soul's value in the marketplace of the world. And so He issued this warning to a hillside crowded with people of faith whose souls were undervalued in favor of outward rule keeping: "What good would it do to get everything you want and lose you, the real you? What could you ever trade your soul for?" (Mark 8:36, MSG). History has proven there are no limits to what "good" men and women will do to get "everything we want," even if it means losing our real self.

Down through the centuries, "selling your soul" has been a chilling theme in lyric and literature. I bartered my soul for the image of a successful Christian leader, even if that man lost sight of God's purposes in his own busyness. Susan bartered (at least) the sense of becoming a solid, mature being who is capable of providing a base from which others can grow for a few moments' appreciation of her personality and career dreams.

A central truth of the Christian life is that, on my own, I do not even know what my desires really are. Someone outside myself who has a spiritual perspective may need to help me see them clearly. Not only that, but I am likely to trade a piece of my soul in exchange for the wrong thing, thinking that "junk food" will feed my craving. Like the prodigal son, I launch out on my own, wanting a free life of self-fulfillment, and wind up eating husks.

The world teaches that we should listen to no one else's agenda for us and independently pursue our dreams. But on our own, our pursuit becomes viciously self-centered and actually destroys our chances of finding the soul's true fulfillment. On our own, our souls become little more than a hungry void, never identifying or finding what it wants. We lose the capacity to know God, to know others, and ironically, to know ourselves. We become self-motivated, self-seeking, and self-centered.

In the end, not only is my connection with God eroded, but my ability to live a fully human life dissolves as well. The ability to truly join my energies to, say, my own child's need for a soul companion to listen and guide is lost. After all, of what importance is my "need" to succeed in business, or in a social circle, or in a ministry, compared to a child's need to learn about life? My ability to give myself to helping an addict recover or a sick person face death is diminished. What can possibly be gained from putting in a string of sixty-hour work weeks to buy the vacation home, or new cars I've wanted, when I have the opportunity to touch lives?

When I sell my soul, seeking my life in outer things, I am reduced to living a superficial existence. I avoid pain and the awkwardness of growing in mutually honest, spiritual relationships, and I instead seek status, gain, and pleasure. Oddly, I may wind up with an impressive title or résumé, but inwardly I know I have lost my identity, little knowing who I really am and where I really belong in the universe, let alone in God's kingdom. I am driven by a fear that the moment I outlive my usefulness, I will not be valued. Or I live with bitter bile in my soul, knowing that my status is based on the upscale neighborhood I live in. Life is reduced to black and white, rather than its living colors. Simple goodness is lost: the encouraging hour with an honest friend, the teachable moment with a child, the cultivation of a creative urge, the "cup of cold water" given to another soul in Jesus' name.

Gradually, the one who is paying out little pieces of his soul becomes one of the "hollow men" that poet T. S. Eliot saw when he looked at modern man. The body and brain keep up the appearance of life, but without the soul, there is no meaning, purpose, joy, peace, authenticity, or experience of God—only a hollow emptiness.

Are you seeking your life in external things? Perhaps you can relate to one of these empty cries of the soul:

- "I work hard to please a perfect God, but never quite measure up. I feel like a perpetual failure. So why keep trying?"
- "I just can't seem to connect with people or God now at a deep level."
- "Sometimes I just get depressed and I don't know why. I ask God to forgive me, but it keeps happening and I can't help it. I have so many questions, doubts, and feelings bottled up inside me. I know that it's wrong. But what am I supposed to do with them?"
- "I'm bored stiff with it all. I've tried every new gimmick, but nothing brings back the excitement I once had for following Christ. I don't know how much longer I can just go through the motions."

Or maybe you can relate to the dryness hidden within these confessions:

- "Life is great. There is always something happening at the kids' schools. My new promotion demands longer hours at work—but I love it. We've become so involved with a couples' group at church that we hardly have time to get out on the new boat. I'm just not sure how long I can keep this pace. Sometimes I even wonder if all of this is what I really want. But I'm too busy to think about that."

■ "It's probably just midlife, but I really feel lost. The kids are off to college, some of our closest friends have divorced. In the midst of it all, God seems to be very distant. It is a lonely and confusing time."

TURNING THE TIDE OF BATTLE

We do not have to live as hollow men and women. We do not have to live with the gnawing emptiness that superficial, self-centered living produces. But we must decide who will best care for our souls—us or God. Only He knows the proper value of our soul and what it is we are exchanging ourselves for.

Jesus directs us to look squarely at the main issue involved here:

"For what will a man be profited, if he gains the whole world, and forfeits his soul? Or what will a man give in exchange for his soul?" (Matthew 16:26)

What will you take in exchange for your soul? A little autonomy from God in which you wind up a slave to some successful image of yourself? What will it profit you to achieve your goal of living free of debt but also devoid of a true relationship with God, your family, and friends who know the real value and needs of your soul?

For thirteen years, Wisconsin Senator William Proxmire has bestowed a "Golden Fleece Award" on government agencies to dramatize examples of wasteful spending. The U.S. Army spent $30,000 for brochures explaining how to play the schoolyard game called "King of the Mountain." The National Institute of Alcoholism spent $102,000 to discover which makes a sunfish more aggressive, gin or tequila.

We rail against wasteful government expenditures. But in light of the eternal importance of our own soul, should we focus so much of our energies into the drive for status, money, possessions, and personal comfort? In the battle to free our souls from a world that would consume us, we give little energy toward seeking what is above.

Investing our energy in what is eternal about us—cultivating the inner person—restores a right order to our lives. It is the greatest investment I can make in my life. And it fortifies my soul against the onslaught of temptations to choose the empty reward.

Three of the gospel writers—Matthew, Mark, and Luke—record an important parable that speaks to cultivating the life within. We know it as the parable of the sower. In it, Jesus depicts four kinds of soil that represent four kinds of people. Each type represents the way people allow the truths that come from God to "penetrate" their lives, or the ways we resist life-changing truth. Consider this parable closely, and honestly consider how it is that you respond to God's efforts of grace to establish His kingdom and life in your soul.

The Resistant Soul

"These are the ones who are beside the road where the word is sown; and when they hear, immediately Satan comes and takes away the word which has been sown in them."
(Mark 4:15)

The "resistant soul" may tolerate living in close proximity to God and His Word, and so it keeps the illusion that hearing the Word of God is the same thing as letting it penetrate to the inner person, where those empowering motives lie. So in place of a heart-to-heart relationship with God, strict theology and morality can function as the outer crust.

In my years as a Christian, and in my work, I have encountered "hard-shelled" individuals who safely exist in a religious system. Charles Dickens created a character like this, "who called her rigidity religion." [3]

None of us is immune from spiritual rigidity. Whenever we set limits on God and what He may or may not do in our lives, we are hardening our hearts to His workings of grace. We are siding with independent self-will and our own motives.

The apostle Paul, quoting God's prophetic word through Isaiah, tells the fate of the resistant soul:

You will keep on hearing, but will not understand; and you will keep on seeing, but will not perceive; for the heart of this people has become dull, and with their ears they scarcely hear, and they have closed their eyes; lest they should see with their eyes, and hear with their ears, and understand with their heart and turn again, and I should heal them. (Acts 28:26-27)

The Shallow Soul

> "In a similar way these are the ones on whom seed is sown on
> the rocky *places*, who, when they hear the word, immediately
> receive it with joy; and they have no *firm* root in themselves
> . . . when affliction or persecution arises . . . immediately they
> fall away." (Mark 4:16-17, emphasis added)

The shallow soul is the one that has never received proper depth of nourishment. How true this can be of the modern Christian whose faith is, in
Bruce Waltke's words, "brain deep, rather than life deep."[4] Perhaps we
come to God and His Word looking for principles to live by so He will
bless us, or answer our prayers. Or we behave morally to keep Him from
getting angry with us. And so the soul relationship with Him remains as
fragile as a sprout in thin, rocky ground.

The shallow soul dies under the weight of life's struggles. Many of
us hope that by becoming Christians we can eliminate struggles and suffering from our lives. How quickly living in a fallen world dashes our
religious illusions! We are called to follow a Lord whose path led through
the crucifixion on the way to resurrection life — who reminds us that in
this world we will have trouble, and the peace we are promised is strength
of soul in adversity (John 16:33).

To experience life and keep my soul requires that I grow in the
knowledge of God that comes only by direct experience of Him. Engag-
ing in the struggles of life with only knowledge about God will result in
defeat. This is what Susan discovered, as we saw earlier. Her shallow
faith was inadequate to help her combat the despair that fell down on her
when the stresses of family life became too great.

Because the shallow soul is unable to trust God in the time of
crisis, the soul is crushed by fear, depression, rejection, abuse, or
discouragement.

The Wandering Soul

> "And others are the ones on whom seed was sown among the
> thorns; these are the ones who have heard the word, and the
> worries of the world, and the deceitfulness of riches, and the
> desires for other things enter in and choke the word, and it
> becomes unfruitful." (Mark 4:18-19)

Acedia is the ancients' word for the condition of soul that comes when we wander from God. This happens when an undue concern for the affairs of life eats out the living heart of faith. The soul that is seduced by the worries of the world, the deceitful lure of riches, or the desire for other things will eventually wander off on the path of apathy toward God.

In this world, we will not only experience trouble, we will never be able to arrange life safely around us, never be able to prevent losses. In this light, worry is the soul's warning that I am preoccupied with a circumstance I have no ultimate control over. As a result, the inner strength that comes from trusting first and only in God is "choked out."

BEWARE SUPERFICIAL ANSWERS

The late Leonard Bernstein observed, speaking of the current culture: "Half of the people are drowned and the other half are swimming in the wrong direction."[5] His observation echoes the ancient cry of Jeremiah. In an era much like our own—punctuated with materialism, greed, rebellion, lack of integrity, and arrogance—Jeremiah cried out on behalf of God about the shallow soul care being offered to His people:

"From the least of them even to the greatest of them, every one is greedy for gain, and from the prophet even to the priest every one deals falsely. And they have healed the wounds of My people slightly, saying, 'Peace, peace,' but there is no peace." (Jeremiah 6:13-14)

The emptiness of the soul of humankind—our "brokenness"—comes from its separation from God. True, we begin again with God when we are first "born" into His family. But this most elemental relationship needs deeper restorations and reconciliation with God. For the empty places in us cry out to be filled, and only true encounter with God will heal, strengthen, and set us on a path that fulfills our humanity in Him.

Recently, I scanned a catalog of religious merchandise and found these otherwise good promises: "steer clear of any real trouble"; "affair-proof your marriage"; "rely on God's power to shed those unwanted pounds"; "regain control of your life"; "break free from the stronghold of sin." The healing claims of books, seminars, and therapies of our day promise much, but often they are not geared to helping us win the soul's real battle, which is to find its way into the spiritual kingdom where God's presence and peace guide us.

Eugene Peterson leads us in a fitting prayer:

> Deliver me, O Lord, from lying lips, from a deceitful tongue. Rescue me from the lies of advertisers who claim to know what I need and what I desire, from the lies of entertainers who promise a cheap way to joy, from the lies of politicians who pretend to instruct me in power and morality, from the lies of psychologists who offer to shape my behavior and my morals so that I will live long, happily and successfully, from the lies of religionists who "heal the wounds of this people lightly," from the lies of moralists who pretend to promote me to the office of captain of my fate, from the lies of pastors who "let go of the commands of God and are holding on to the traditions of men" (Mark 7:8, NIV). Rescue me from the person who tells me of life and omits Christ, who is wise in the ways of the world and ignores the movement of the Spirit.[6]

If your desire is reflected in this prayer, then your soul is "good soil"—a soul in which the Word of God and the character of Christ can root and grow.

RESTORATION

At the council of Jerusalem, Peter described a situation which continues to this day: "placing upon the neck of the disciples a yoke which neither our fathers nor we have been able to bear" (Acts 15:10). The yoke of religious duty produces the "unsettling [of] your souls" (verse 24) rather than the inner rest and purposeful outer direction that results from being joined to God in Christ.

Training our souls to seek God, in the childlike confidence of Christ our brother, brings refreshment as we are restored to fellowship with God. Otherwise, we find ourselves trying one dry dead end after another, just like the fictional character Jill in C. S. Lewis's fanciful work, *The Silver Chair.*

Jill is nearly dying of thirst when she hears the rippling of a stream. She comes within sight of the clear, delicious-looking water, only to find that a huge lion—Aslan, the Christ figure—lies menacingly beside it. The intensity of Jill's thirst is matched only by her fear of the lion. She asks Aslan to go away long enough to let her drink. He refuses. She asks him to promise not to hurt her. He says, "I make no promise." Desperate, she insists she will simply find another stream—to which Aslan replies, "There is no other stream."[7]

How much are we like Jill—wanting the thirst of our souls quenched on our own terms? We ask the Lord to step back, so we can fill our souls with His blessings without dealing with Him. We look to God to protect us from hurt and trouble, while we insist on remaining in control of the direction of our lives.

What we need is to let Him enter inside the soul's invisible walls of fear and pride, which continue to keep Him out of the center of our lives.

WE NEED HIS HELP TO GO ON FROM HERE

To win the battle for our souls, we need to allow God full access to all that is in us. We need to stop resisting Him and learn how to relax and trust Him to do the deeper work in us.

And yet, we come to the real battle line: Rather than encounter God in the depths of our being, we prefer to avoid Him. It is at this point we need to listen to Jesus calling us: Come to Me . . . learn from Me . . . and you will find restoration for your souls (Matthew 11:28,29). We need His Spirit to help us here, to cross over from a life that is withering because it is continually centered in ourselves, to a life that is growing because it is being restored from within. As the 17th century Scottish pastor, Samuel Rutherford, discovered:

> I can let Christ grip me, but I cannot grip him. I love to be kissed, and to sit on Christ's knee; but I cannot set my feet to the ground, for afflictions bring the cramp upon my faith. All that I can do is hold out a lame faith to Christ like a beggar holding out a stump, instead of an arm or leg, and cry, "Lord Jesus, work a miracle!" O what I would give to have hands and arms to grip strongly and fold handsomely about Christ's neck, and to have my claim made good with real possession![8]

What Rutherford knew is this: Ultimately, God Himself is at work to help us win the battle to keep our souls on the right path of growth and maturity. With that in mind, let's turn our attention to some of the ways God guides our souls deeper into Him.

CHAPTER FOUR

GOD'S WAYS IN SOUL KEEPING

Eye has not seen and ear has not heard . . . all that God has prepared for those who love Him.

1 CORINTHIANS 2:9

The soul is capable of much more than we can imagine.[1]

TERESA OF AVILA

Many of us are taught that becoming a Christian is the arrival point. Initially, this gives a great sense of security to the new Christian.

But A.W. Tozer describes quite well the plight such thinking brings us to eventually:

> Everything is made to center upon the initial act of "accepting" Christ . . . and we are not expected thereafter to crave any further revelation of God to our souls. We have been snared in the coils of a spurious logic which insists that if we have found Him, we need no more seek Him.[2]

Scripture describes the believer as a pilgrim on the way to a better country, not a settler who has arrived in the Promised Land (see Hebrews 11:13-16). The biblical and classical image of "journey" provides a robust metaphor for the life of faith. It captures the sense of movement, purpose, and destination that make up the Christian life. This can be very unsettling when you have it in your head that you've arrived at the end, rather than having discovered that life in Christ is the right beginning.

If the concept of a journey of growth is new for you, it may be helpful to think in terms of the difference between a wedding and a marriage. When a couple comes together, the wedding ceremony is not the goal, it is an act symbolizing the start of something new. After that, the couple will need to understand how to make a life together in all of life's circumstances. They will need to know more about each other's motives, loves and hates, and how the other accomplishes things. Similarly, becoming a Christian is the beginning of a process in which we come to understand God's will for us, and His way of working to direct us.

What is hard for many of us to accept is this: The journey of faith will take us through the many changing conditions of the soul. We may not have expected things to get tougher before they get better. Certainly, we did not expect to have our innermost selves exposed—our misgivings about God, our doubt, apathy, disillusionment, depression. Because many of us think like people who are supposed to have arrived, we do not think of these as interior conditions God may lead us through to show us greater glimpses of Himself.

We need to accept that spiritual growth is not only a journey, but God Himself is leading us in it—through times of challenge and darkness, as well as times of ease and blessing. We have only to think of the biblical heroes to see that God determines times of struggle along with times of clarity.

Moses spent years in the silence of the Midian wilderness; Joseph languished, his prayers unanswered, while he sat in an Egyptian prison; Ruth felt the desperation of loneliness after the death of her husband; David nearly despaired of life while enemies sought to kill him as he hid in caves; Jonah felt abandoned by God in the belly of a fish; Job was lost in painful confusion after living a righteous life and watching all his blessings be destroyed; Jeremiah was betrayed and shamed by God's people after speaking the truth. Consider your current situation in light of the way God accomplished His deeper purposes in these lives.

Perhaps you experienced a time of blessing after committing your life to Christ. Now it is time to ask yourself a challenging question: "Is it possible that what I am experiencing at this very moment is a piece of the journey that is part of the plan of a wise, good, and loving God? Could it be that God is as interested in developing my faith as He was in developing that of Moses, Ruth, and Joseph?"

GETTING BEYOND "STUCK"

When we fail to allow God into the picture, we remain stuck right where we are—wherever that may be.

Recently, I spent time with a thirty-five-year-old missionary, home on furlough and suffering a terrible bout with depression. He was suffering, not only because (as it turned out) something painful was buried in his soul, but he was also depressed about being depressed. Because of his early Christian training, he saw his depression as a "sinful state" that reflected spiritual weakness. As we talked it became clear that God was bringing wounds and anger from the past to the surface—feelings he was able to become aware of while on furlough since he had the space in his life to pay attention to his soul's movements.

I suggested he view this confusing time as part of a journey designed by God to get at deeper issues. This was a new thought, but he promised to spend time alone, opening himself to this possibility.

When we spoke again, he had indeed found freedom in accepting his current condition as a "place" God had led him to. In fact, he felt grateful that God had seemed to arrange pressures and losses in his life, so he would have to focus on important matters of the soul—things that were keeping him from growing closer to God and other people, actually hindering him in his work. He was amazed to experience God's grace right in the very heart of depression and that God could draw him closer to Himself by acting directly upon his soul.

Up to that point, he'd been stuck for months, more concerned about outwardly conforming to the image of what a "good Christian" looks like than allowing God to inwardly transform him. But in this intimate, reshaping way, God does involve Himself with us, and if we accept His work in us, He can show a little more of His glory through us in very particular ways.

Highway of the Heart

Paul affirms the truth that it is God who is at work to influence us as we make our way through this life (1 Corinthians 3:6). What we can do to help ourselves is to recognize His movements. And we can learn, too, how to respond to God out of our souls in the manner of our Lord and example, Jesus. Let's consider this more closely.

Jesus proclaimed that the life of faith is a journey when He told us, "I am the way" (John 14:6). The Greek word for "way" is *odos,* from which we get our words "odometer" and "exodus." Just as the exodus was God's decisive saving act for Israel, so Jesus is our "exodus"—our way through our soul's bondage and confusion and into the spiritual freedom that comes under the direction of God. The early disciples responded to the call of Jesus and were known as people of the Way (Acts 9:2) before they were called Christians (Acts 11:26). The Christian faith was simply known as "the Way" throughout the book of Acts (9:2; 19:9,23; 22:4; 24:14,22).

Individually and as members of Christ's body, the church, we are people of "the way"—people who are walking the spiritual path with God, in the same open, directable spirit that Christ demonstrated. Being a spiritual pilgrim defines who I am and what my life is about. Though I may possess a home and pursue a career to use my skills, my life is not ultimately about success, status, accumulation, or happiness. Rather, it is about keeping my soul alive and moving on the path God has for me. It is about growing until I reach the journey's end, to which I am called by God.

Christians are often told that the end goal of following God in Christ is something like this: "to live a good, moral life," or "to live without worries," or "to go to heaven." These are inadequate and less than biblical notions of the soul's highest end.

The true goal is captured by the visionary apostle John:

Beloved, now we are children of God, and it has not appeared as yet what we shall be. We know that, when He appears, we shall be like Him, because we shall see Him just as He is. (1 John 3:2)

To see Christ face-to-face, "just as He is," means far more than "putting a face to a name." This is what we say when we meet someone to whom we've spoken on the phone but never met in person. John implies something deeper: to see Him face-to-face means that the true "face" of my soul—all of the attitudes and expressions I may have hidden within me, masked by the face I put on in public—will meet the attitudes of God as shown in Christ. Then my soul will understand fully for the first time all that was in God's heart toward me, all that He meant to accomplish by what He led me through in my life. Then awe, joy, and gratitude will melt away my final resistance, and we will become, at last, spiritually one.

As I progress on the spiritual journey, there is a quiet transformation that occurs in my life—God occurs in my life. God seems to change, but in reality, I am the one who has changed. This is beautifully illustrated in this exchange between Aslan, the lion Christ-figure, and the young girl Lucy from C. S. Lewis' Chronicles of Narnia:

"Welcome, child," he said.

"Aslan," said Lucy, "you're bigger."

"That is because you are older, little one," answered he.

"Not because you are?"

"I am not. But every year you grow, you will find me bigger."[3]

As we grow in our love for Christ, experience of Christ, and obedience in Christ, He looms larger and larger so that we can begin to say with the apostle Paul, "For me to live is Christ." And we gladly join John the Baptist in proclaiming, "He must increase, I must decrease."

Until that day, our journey is to experience the character and presence of the living Christ ever deepening in us.

NOT YOUR USUAL KIND OF TRIP

The problem with our spiritual growth is that it does not happen in a logical fashion. That would make it simpler. But logical and simpler are not always better. And they do not appear to be God's way.

Consider this: Many people fail miserably, make an absolute mess of things, and reach the proverbial end of the line (or bottom of the barrel) before they come to themselves and find their way again. In this indirect and illogical way, they finally make deeper connections to God.

A road trip we once made helped me to make sense of this.

We had to travel from our home in Colorado to California to take our daughter to college in Santa Barbara. This involved going around mountains and deserts. Because of that, we chose a route that was not exactly the shortest. At times we were actually driving in a southeastern direction, when Santa Barbara was to the northwest.

This struck me as a true map of the lives of many people. I have known enthusiastic Christians who set out to follow Christ and work hard at being perfect, or at least very good people. But it seems that one thing after another falls in their path to frustrate and bring out the worst in them. Ultimately, under the external pressure of hardships and the internal pressure to "appear" unflappable and loving, they crack. In discouragement and anger at God, who seems to have weighed them down with an impossible task, they utterly give up. They cry, "I want to follow You, but I can't do this. Not unless You show me how."

That is when they seem to hear God's voice telling them He has been trying to get them to this point of abandonment to Him and His strength all along.

By taking a path through hard work, ultimately God brings them to an understanding of interior rest and the empowerment of grace.

Do you see what I'm getting at? We aim at one destination: to be people who are good and spiritual. God wants to get us there, too. But first, it seems, He must lead us by an opposite, or indirect, route, working humility and peace and carefree, childlike obedience into our resistant soul.

A second thought came to me as I considered our trek to California: Had we not known our destination, it would have seemed like we were lost or pathetically misdirected at times. But because we knew where we had to wind up, we could tolerate the brief times when we had to head south in order to go north.

Such is our stubborn human nature that, when we are desperate and lost, we are most willing to surrender to new perspectives on life and accept new directives. If we understand how such times help us arrive at our ultimate destination, we can begin to make room for them as normal, and even necessary, passages in our spiritual growth. As Bernard of Clairvaux wrote in the 12th century, "When you have heard what the reward is, the labor of the climb will be less."[4]

The apostle Paul understood these principles of soul keeping, and he reminds us that God "causes all things to work together" to conform us to the image of God's Son (Romans 8:28-29). Often these verses are used in a shallow way, meaning, "If you look hard enough, you'll see that some good circumstance results from your terrible loss." This is silly superficiality. We may never see "earthly good" from losses we suffer in this lifetime. The "good" that Paul refers to in this passage is God's purpose of conforming us to the image of Christ.

If we do not want to get lost in our circumstances, we must take this attitude: Nothing is outside the reach of God's redemptive work, even if we can see no redeeming value in it right now. Only then can we view every circumstance as an opportunity to have the spirit of Christ formed in us.

GROWING STAGES

I have offered some views about the nature of the Christian's spiritual journey. It will be helpful now to give you an idea of the changes you will encounter in yourself, perhaps again and again, deepening in spirit each time.

Janet Hagberg and Robert Guelich in their book, *The Critical Journey*, do as fine a job as any contemporary writers of exploring six stages of the soul's growth. As it happens they fit my story well, so I will weave my personal experience into the stages to help illustrate them.

Stage One: Recognition of God

As the only child of churchgoing parents, I attended a small-town church where I developed an image of God as Rule Giver, Score Keeper, and Judge. This understanding prevailed until my fifth-grade year, when my dad needed drastic surgery to remove cancer from his jaw and tongue. Dad's cancer caused us to draw together to pray as a family for the first time. When Dad survived the crisis, it produced in me an image of a God who was personal, caring, and who answered prayer.

But I wondered what demands God placed on me in return for His kindness. I felt that I "owed" Him. Through high school my relationship with God was characterized by guilt and fear of punishment. I bargained with Him on several occasions to get me out of tight spots, promising that I would never sin again. By graduation, my desire to please God had waned.

As you see, in this first stage, a distinct image of God develops, along with certain ways of relating to this image. Hagberg and Guelich's observation is that we are drawn to God through a sense of either need or awe. For me it was the sense of need, while others are drawn by the majesty of creation, or perhaps inspiring worship. This beginning of faith is undeveloped, innocent, and simply sincere.

Stage Two: Commitment to Following God

Though I made a commitment to God in grade school, I didn't experience a personal relationship with Jesus until my freshman year in college. For the next twenty years my spiritual growth and fellowship would come primarily through Young Life, a mission of evangelism to adolescents. The focus of my four years in college and an additional four years in seminary was on learning about God through the Scriptures. Objective truth was paramount. Every question required an answer; every problem could be solved. Being "right" was important, and there was an "us versus them" attitude between those of us who had the truth and those who didn't. I finished seminary in 1978 with a love for the Scriptures, a rigid faith, a wonderful wife, a two-month-old daughter, and a wealth of knowledge about God—but a dearth of firsthand experience of God Himself.

During this stage, individuals tend to find security and identity in a leader, a group, or a belief system. The core of faith at this time is learning about God through the Scriptures.

Stage Three: The Productive Life

After graduating from seminary, I was eager to use my accumulated knowledge to do great things for God. Preserving some time for family life, I gave the rest of my energy to ministry. I operated on the basis that God would bless hard work, so ministry effectiveness was very much up to me. This introduced an anxiety into my work that drained the life out of my relationship with God. I also believed God to be a difficult taskmaster who was never quite pleased. Gradually, imperceptibly, I became angry with God for what I felt was His inaction in my life and ministry. God had become the means to the end, which for me was success in ministry. Even spiritual exercises and disciplines were done because they were the required duties if God was to "work." Though I experienced apparent success in my work, there was little fulfillment, much frustration, shallow relationships, insecurity in ministry, and dryness in my life with God.

For many, this stage starts as a time of finding a place of service to God. Yet in time, it can become a cage. People feel stuck in an unfulfilling role, yet they feel they are letting God down or abandoning the work He has called them to do. So they continue to live in a dull, gray weariness on a treadmill of performance.

Stage Four: The Journey Inward

Though my life was well-ordered and disciplined, I was too busy serving God to take the time to really know Him. In the famous words of Dante's *Inferno*, I had come to the middle of life and "I found myself astray in a dark wood."[5]

Success no longer seemed to satisfy. Failures created deep disillusionment. I was forced to look inward. There I faced a gnawing emptiness that refused to be filled. For two years I tried everything but could not escape the growing cold inside. Then in January of 1990, I had the opportunity to attend the three-day silent retreat I mentioned earlier. A small bit of light began to break through. My whole life was turned upside down as the result of experiencing the reality of Jesus and His unchanging love for me. My new passion was for intimacy with God, rather than service for Him. What it required, though, was the surrendering of my egocentric needs for success and significance. It was like a second conversion.

Most often, the inner journey is precipitated by some sort of crisis, either internal or external. The old certainties no longer work, and the search is on for a new direction. This can be a dark and painful phase of spiritual growth. John of the Cross described an intense version of this stage as a "dark night of the soul." We may not experience those depths, but we can expect to be led by the Holy Spirit to turn inward and discover the love and power of the indwelling Christ.

The inner journey leads us to discover more of our true selves. Many Christians balk at this idea, thinking it is self-centered, while at the same time they are driven by motivations they themselves do not see and which make life difficult. The inward look helps us see we have a good deal to turn over to God in order for Him to change us. This takes time. It took me a couple of years to discover what God was showing me about my self-centered drives, aimed at bringing praise to myself, and then about three years for God to restore my soul as I learned various spiritual pathways that rebuild the inner man, like those we will look at here. (Of course, the process continues into eternity.)

Stage Five: The Journey Outward

Eventually, we are ready to journey outward from a new and deeper foundation, which comes with the sense that we are surrendering the inner person and its hidden motivations to the will of God; that is, from a new foundation in Christ. For me, inner changes led to a change of vocation.

The outer journey can look very similar to the earlier life of production, but the energy and motivation are completely different now. In my case, I am no longer striving to accomplish great things for God, but I am learning to recognize God's awesome ways of working in people's lives, to cooperate with Him in ministering to them. I am also more relaxed about surrendering to His higher purposes when circumstances go against me. The journey outward proceeds from a sense of living out of a deep center, which is God's presence in you.

A person in this stage experiences a profound peace and takes delight in simply being God's person, able to see God in all aspects of life. He or she can seem to have a carelessness about things that others consider important—like image and career success—because he or she enjoys the restful surrender to God of his or her future, family, finances, status, and significance.

Stage Six: The Life of Love

The life of love is one caught up in loving God, and as a result, loving all others for His sake. It is, again, expressed by the apostle Paul in his proclamation, "For me to live is Christ, and to die is gain" (Philippians 1:21). Many Christians may momentarily experience this kind of life, but it seems few are willing to abandon self so completely that their life becomes a vessel of God's life.

It is difficult to describe these fully-surrendered people who live the life of love. They are simply vessels who have been filled by the Holy Spirit with the character of Christ, and they see everyone as an object of God's intense sacrificial love. Almost naturally they lay down their lives—because their lives are not their own—following the example of Jesus.

Keep in mind that what I am speaking of here is an ideal, a phase of your growth that comes with time. Expect to see this kind of love coming out in certain areas of your life before it becomes habitual in all relationships. Remember, the most profound, lasting transformations take time—and God gives us both time and grace as He works to change us.

RHYTHMS OF THE SOUL

Another helpful way to view the spiritual journey is to see God working, perhaps not in stages, but in "rhythms."

Christians of the past speak of the rhythms of spiritual growth, which God Himself allows. These rhythms have been known as "consolation" and "desolation." In his great work, *The Spiritual Exercises,* Ignatius observes that these "peaks and valleys" of soul are integral to spiritual growth.[6] Not only should we expect them, they are apparently necessary.

Consolation is the term that simply means to enjoy the sense or knowledge of God's presence. We are not necessarily talking about warm feelings or "supernatural chills." But there are times when we are deeply aware of God's love, strength, grace, and blessing. To experience a time of consolation does not necessarily mean that all is well in our circumstances. Some of the richest times of consolation for my soul have been at times of outward loss, disappointment, or failure. That is when God's gracious, loving presence has been the most real. Most of us can recall experiencing varying degrees of spiritual consolation, and some of these may even be of the "mountaintop" variety.

What is more difficult to accept are the times of spiritual desolation. These are the times when, due to no fault of our own, God seems distant or absent. This is hard for many Christians who have ingrained in their minds the bumper-sticker theology that says, "If you don't feel close to God, guess who moved?"

How is it that I may be aware of God's presence, love, and work in my life—even if only in a general way—and then one day it is as if I stepped into a void? For most Christians who experience this, the tendency is to continue in their regular spiritual practices—praying, reading Scripture, and attending church. They are hoping these "old faithful" habits will jump-start their spiritual life again, only to find that nothing works. There is no sense of God's presence, a disinterest in the Scriptures, and hollowness in prayer. Then deeper dismay might fall upon them, and spiritual desolation.

But the spiritual masters assure us that God may indeed withdraw the evidence of His presence—but not really withdraw Himself from us. It is as if He merely draws a thin veil between us. God's purpose, it is thought, is to help us let go of the need for spiritual feelings, which many of us build our spiritual lives on or use as a gauge. This purifies us of the need for sensual feelings and intensifies our desire for Him alone. When I consistently experience God's blessings, it is only natural that I become attached to those "consolations" rather than to the God who gives them. When the sense of God's presence is withdrawn, my heart's desire for the Lord can grow more passionate. Many psalms of lament are cries to God for help from the wilds of spiritual desolation.

This rhythm of consolation and desolation parallels the dual nature of our journey's destination, *communion with Christ* and *likeness to Christ*. In consolation I experience new depths of communion with Christ. In desolation I am challenged to greater humility, surrender, and obedience, and I am transformed in soul to be more like Christ. In consolation I am drawing near to Christ. In desolation I am letting go of everything but Christ.

TOWARD GOD

Though these movements and rhythms are surely not experienced by all Christians, they do seem fairly common among those serious about following the Lord. As the Spirit of God draws us higher and closer to Himself, there are several directional movements that we can notice and cooperate with. We may sense ourselves moving:

- from impulsive action to listening in prayer
- from control to surrender
- from self-sufficiency to poverty of spirit
- from working for God to letting God work through me
- from many false selves to my one true self in Christ
- from external acts of righteousness to walking in faith, hope, and love
- from initiating to responding
- from seeing God in me to seeing us in God
- from individualism to community
- from personal goals to communion with God

If you sense yourself being moved in these directions, you can be confident that you are cooperating with God's work of soul keeping. Be assured that you are headed toward your soul's "destination."

And now let's proceed on to some of the most important pathways of the soul.

PART TWO

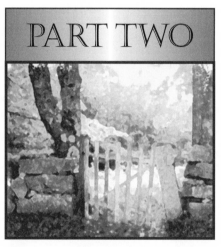

THE ANCIENT
PATHS

CHAPTER FIVE

GRACE: THE PATH THROUGH GUILT

"The prodigal said, 'I will get up and go to my father, and will say to him, "Father, I have sinned against heaven, and in your sight; I am no longer worthy to be called your son; make me as one of your hired men."' And he got up and came to his father. But while he was still a long way off, his father saw him, and felt compassion for him, and ran and embraced him, and kissed him."

LUKE 15:18-20

Nobody will be kicked out for having a rotten life, because nobody there will have any life but the life of Jesus. God will say to everybody, You were dead and are alive again; you were lost and are found: put on a funny hat and step inside.

ROBERT CAPON[1]

The grace of God means something like: Here is your life. You might never have been, but you are because the party wouldn't have been complete without you.

FREDERICK BUECHNER[2]

The first time I knew I didn't measure up was in the second grade. Along with the rest of my friends, I joined the school glee club because I enjoyed singing. But the teacher wasn't enjoying my off-key attempts. There would be an audition, she said, to see if we "deserved" to be in the club. I didn't make the cut. Later efforts in baseball tryouts, spelling bees, and school had better results. But they only validated the first message in a different way: I am judged on performance.

This is the world of performance-demands in which we all grew up. Ask people the question, "Who in your life has loved you unconditionally?" Most are stumped. It is outside the range of their experience.

This is why the message of Jesus is "good news." It is a gospel of the unconditional love of God for each of us. Yet the message heard by many is bad news of a religion that offers the pleasure of God's help for the well behaved and hard working. Good news becomes bad news when something important is left out — that something is the empowering grace of God. Without grace, our spirituality can cast us into a life of anxiety, worthlessness, uncertainty. Without grace, we avoid real encounters with God and are stuck in a state of depression.

Maybe you can identify with the feelings of these people:

- Anxiety: "Sure, I know that God loves me and forgives me, but people are a different story. I am so afraid of doing the wrong thing, of messing up. How do I get out of this anxiety that I live with every day?"
- Worthlessness: "Our finances are in bad shape. I should have never changed jobs — another stupid decision. I can't do anything right. My wife and children deserve so much better. Everything builds up inside of me — this feeling of not being worth anything — and I get depressed."

- Uncertainty: "Sometimes I wonder if I'm really a Christian. Why can't God speak to me the way He did to Paul on the Damascus road? Then I could be sure."
- Dryness: "I am just tired of trying to be a Christian. I have no more enthusiasm for this. *None.*"
- Depression: "I cannot go to God once more admitting I'm down. After all, He died on the cross for me, and I should be joyful. Isn't depression a terrible sin? I mean, in light of what God has done for me, isn't it terrible of me to be down so much of the time?"

Each one comes from a man or woman who appears to know little about God's open path of learning and grace. Some have been led by legalistic teachers, very much like the Galatians were, whom Paul addressed in the New Testament. Having begun "by the Spirit" we can be misled to sidestep the way of grace and follow a "different gospel" of spiritual works and formulas. Maybe the majority of Christians never really grasp the reality that our whole relationship with God from beginning to end is a gift, and the steps we follow make up a pathway through the heart, laid out by God Himself.

So many of the Church's best spiritual directors and teachers begin by guiding souls in their care into the path of grace. It is impossible to single out just one step, so we will look at a composite of the most important ones. We are speaking here of heart attitudes, not merely "ten easy steps to walking in grace."

ENEMIES OF GRACE

First, it is necessary to look at the forces that oppose this gift of God. When the only operating mode we know is to work hard to remain in God's favor, the enemies of grace will invade our lives.

What follows is a list of what A.W. Tozer called the "hyphenated sins of the human spirit"[3]:

Self-Righteousness

We are right to condemn the Pharisees' pride and blindness. They saw themselves as guardians of the truth and protectors of public morality, but inwardly they were miserably trapped in an effort to prove themselves to God. Does this sound familiar?

The Pharisee is adept at working a system and lives with a sense of being trapped in a religious life whose demands he cannot satisfy. He fears leaving God's service mostly because he is afraid that God will punish him by allowing things to fall apart emotionally, financially, and relationally. He believes he is only "blessed" as a result of his obedience to God's principles, and receiving more grace for the future will be his reward if he puts out great efforts to live a godly life. Pharisees, both modern and ancient, fail to see that even their ability to work is a gift and that they were blessed before they ever had a chance to earn anything. Or as Augustine put it, "We did not exist when we were predestined, we were hostile when we were called, and we were sinners when we were justified."[4]

Self-righteousness is not the fruit of grace, but of the religion of self-help.

Self-Defeat

We defeat ourselves when we try to bear the impossible burden of "pleasing" God. We defeat ourselves when we fail to draw on the ever-present help of God to lift and empower us.

The tax collectors and sinners of Jesus' day knew they had no chance of being included in God's Kingdom. This is why Jesus' open welcome to all was such good news to the defeated, the destitute, and the discouraged. No one is good enough to earn entrance into the Kingdom, yet as a gift, God's presence is near to each one of us, if we will turn to Him.

We defeat ourselves by failing to run to God for the grace of His help every moment we need it.

Self-Contempt

I have met many men and women who feel like stepchildren in God's family. These well-meaning believers are more conscious of their sin than they are of their Savior. When asked how God is at work in their lives, they would rarely mention His presence, soul training, love, or encouragement. Rather, they would speak of seeing mostly sin, failure, and weakness. Their resolve, which originates in guilt and shame, is to redouble efforts and try harder to be pleasing to God. And the cycle of work-and-eventual-failure goes on, with ever-increasing self-contempt.

Perhaps this is why Paul was so confrontational with the Galatians, calling them "bewitched," "foolish," and "fallen from grace." He knew that the treadmill of "spiritual performance" leads only to tiredness without progress. And eventually, to condemning ourselves all over again.

Whether the enemy is self-righteousness, self-defeat, or self-contempt, the result is that our soul loses its way on the true path to God. It is as if our spiritual nerve endings lose feeling, and we quickly lose touch in our relationship with a loving God.

WHERE ALL PATHS BEGIN

All aspects of creation, redemption, and holy living start with a gift from God. For the Christian, grace is where everything begins.

Jesus opened His public ministry by reading these words:

"The Spirit of the Lord is upon Me, because He anointed Me
to preach the gospel to the poor. He has sent Me to proclaim
release to the captives, and recovery of sight to the blind, to
set free those who are downtrodden, to proclaim the favorable
year of the Lord." (Luke 4:18-19)

Later, Jesus would say He had come to seek and save the lost. Watching Him relate to the "lost," the enemies of grace referred to Jesus in a derogatory way as a "friend of tax-gatherers and sinners." In fact, this description was well deserved. Jesus sided with a woman caught in adultery and pulled Matthew, the money-grubbing tax collector, to His side — all the while announcing that the Kingdom of God would be found by those who understood they were "poor in spirit."

Have you noticed that truly good news — say, the birth of a child or news of a promotion or a clean bill of health — always lifts the soul? That is why the broken and hurting followed Jesus around by the thousands. They were hearing good news of forgiveness, freedom, love, and joy in the kingdom of God. The credo of Young Life is this: "It's a sin to bore a kid with the gospel." If it's boring, it's probably not the gospel of grace. Rules, regulations, moral codes, and performance standards are boring — but good news of acceptance, release, help, and freedom for the soul is breathtaking.

That is the gospel of grace offered to you and to me.

THE RIGHT TAKEOFF

Grace provides the daily strength for the Christian's spiritual journey. The believer begins a relationship with God as one who is accepted, loved, and delighted in. Much as a new mother beams with joy when the infant is first placed in her arms, so God delights in each of us as a proud Father (Psalm 18:19). In the security of unconditional love I am free to grow and develop in my life with God. I am not hindered by a need to win approval because it has been freely given. I am not entangled by doubts of my worthiness, for God gives me worth in Christ. If God is for me, who can be against me? It is God who has declared me righteous; who can condemn me (Romans 8:31; 33-34)?

The extravagant generosity of our gracious God is seen in the parable of the "generous landowner" (see Matthew 20). Jesus' main theme is that grace is the modus operandi of God's Kingdom because the laborers who worked for an hour were paid the same as those who had worked all day. The rewards come out of the landowner's generosity, not as a result of the quantity of the laborers' work. Obviously, this would present problems to Christians in a capitalist culture. John Chrysostom's homily on this passage draws us into this kingdom of grace:

> Enter then, all of you into the joy of our Lord. First and last, receive alike your reward. Rich and poor, dance together. You who have fasted and you who have not fasted, rejoice today. The table is fully laden; let all enjoy it. The calf is fatted; let none go away hungry. Let none lament his poverty; for the universal Kingdom is revealed. Let none bewail his transgressions; for the light of forgiveness has risen from the tomb. Let none fear death; for the death of the Savior has set us free.[5]

Fyodor Dostoyevsky, perhaps the greatest novelist of all time, spoke poignantly of grace through one of the characters from *Crime and Punishment*, a drunken father of a prostitute who said,

> At the last Judgment Christ will say to us, "Come, you also! Come, drunkards! Come, weaklings! Come, children of shame!" And he will say to us: "Vile beings, you who are in the image of the beast and bear his mark, but come all the

same, you as well." And the wise and prudent will say, "Lord, why do you welcome them?" And he will say: "If I welcome them, you wise men, if I welcome them, you prudent men, it is because not one of them has ever been judged worthy." And he will stretch out his arms, and we will fall at his feet, and we will cry out sobbing, and then we will understand all, we will understand the Gospel of grace! Lord, your Kingdom come![6]

Some may object, saying that this overstates the gospel of grace. Is this possible—when we have a Savior who, from the cross, asked the Father to forgive the very ones who crucified Him? Though it is beyond our comprehension, this magnificent grace is at the heart of our faith.

BECOMING THE BELOVED

To walk in grace is to allow ourselves the experience of being loved by Christ. Though it sounds easy, opening ourselves to the love of another can be a risky proposition. The apostle John, the disciple whom Jesus loved, leads us on this path.

The book of John, chapter thirteen, records events on the night before Jesus was crucified. He gathered His disciples for one last time of fellowship around a table and to memorialize His imminent death and resurrection. Following His incredible act of love and humility in washing the feet of the disciples, Jesus predicted that one of them would betray Him. This prompted suspicious looks and quiet questions among all of the disciples except one—John. While the others were relying on their understanding to try to ascertain the identity of the betrayer, John was leaning on the breast of Jesus in devoted affection. What a picture this is!

Brennan Manning, in his testament of grace, *Abba's Child*, judges this scene to be the defining moment of John's life. Certainly John saw it that way, for from that moment on in his gospel he refers to himself as the "disciple whom Jesus loved" (see John 13:23; 19:26; 20:2; 21:7,20).

The effects of experiencing the love of Jesus are immediately evident in John's life. He was the only disciple at the cross (John 19:26-30). He was first to the tomb and first to believe in the resurrection (John 20:1-9). He was the first to recognize the Risen Jesus (John 21:1-14). And he was the first to follow the resurrected Lord (John 21:15-25).

If we are willing to be people "whom Jesus loves" we will see the same effects in our lives. Just as John did, we will gladly share in the sufferings of Christ. The experience of being loved will strengthen our faith, just as it did for John. It will give us spiritual insight to recognize Jesus in surprising places. And finally, when we are loved and know it, we will follow Jesus, just as John did. In fact, when we know we are loved, we follow not as a disciple or as a servant, but as a beloved in passionate pursuit of the Lover of our souls.

Here are some insights from John's first epistle to us, his manifesto of love:

- ■ 1 John 2:10: The one who loves his brother abides in the light and there is no cause for stumbling in him.
- ■ 1 John 3:1: See how great a love the Father has bestowed upon us, that we should be called children of God.
- ■ 1 John 3:16: We know love by this, that He laid down His life for us.
- ■ 1 John 3:18: Little children, let us not love with word or with tongue, but in deed and truth.
- ■ 1 John 4:7: Beloved, let us love one another, for love is from God; and everyone who loves is born of God and knows God.
- ■ 1 John 4:8: The one who does not love does not know God, for God is love.
- ■ 1 John 4:18: There is no fear in love, but perfect love casts out fear.
- ■ 1 John 4:19: We love, because He first loved us.

These words of love were written some sixty years after John had leaned his head on Jesus, becoming the beloved. He never recovered from the experience. Or as it has been said, "The one who has the disease called Jesus will never be cured." How, then, do we catch this passionate joy that comes from knowing the love of God for us?

EMBRACED BY GRACE

When we surrender to the embrace of grace, we relax in knowing we are the beloved of God. I want to offer you two stories that give us glimpses of the embrace of grace.

As a Christmas present, when he was eleven, my son Cody received a BB gun. A few days later, my wife and I were going out for the evening and left Cody at home with his friend. They decided to get out their BB guns to do some target practice from his bedroom window. What they didn't know was that when they missed their target, they were hitting the neighbors' window. The neighbors assumed vandalism and called the police. Two terrified boys, one hysterical mother, and some puzzled neighbors greeted us when we returned home. As the conference broke up, I walked outside with Cody. In tears, he buried his head in my chest and said, "Dad, I'm so sorry." I had never loved him more than I did at that moment as I wrapped my arms around him. To that point in his young life, it was his biggest failure, yet even as a sinful, earthly father, my heart was drawn to him as never before. How much more does the heart of our heavenly Father reach out to us when we are bruised?

That question is answered in Jesus' story of the prodigal son in Luke 15. The younger son had rejected his father, squandered his inheritance, and become destitute. It occurred to him that maybe he could go back home and be hired as a field hand. He prepared his speech and headed home. Before he could get a word out—"while he was still a long way off"—his father saw him, was moved with compassion, and ran to embrace and kiss him.

This is the clearest picture that you will find of your heavenly Father: a God who has been looking for you for a long time. The dynamo of His great heart is powered by compassion. When He sees you turning from the world and your confusion to look for Him, He runs to you. Though you feel awkward in His embrace, aware as you are that your soul is not "clean," He seems not to notice, and presses His lips to your face. With no word spoken, you understand that His very Spirit is one of forgiveness, and all debts are canceled.

Isn't this what we mean when we sing about amazing grace?

WALKING THE PATH OF GRACE

If you are a Christian at all, it is because of grace. Jesus said that no one could come to Him without the Father first drawing him (John 6:44). The first movement toward God is itself the gift of God. The apostle Paul removes all doubt concerning the origin and means of salvation when he says, "For by grace you have been saved through faith; and that not of yourselves, *it is* the gift of God" (Ephesians 2:8, emphasis added).

Grace is where we started in the Christian life, but as Robert Capon noticed, "at the first opportunity we run from its strange light . . . straight back to the familiar darkness of the law."[7] In Revelation 2:1-7, Jesus rebukes the Ephesian church and implores them to "remember from where you have fallen." Like the Galatians before them, the Ephesians had left their first love relationship with God and turned to dutiful works.

The person who walks this path will live with a growing awareness that he or she is the beloved of God. This is our challenge. To keep yourself growing in a spirit of grace, you may wish to make the following practices part of your life.

Remember

Jesus asks the Ephesians, the Galatians, and us to remember when He invited us to drink from the water of life without cost and our spiritual thirst was quenched. Remember how we felt loved, forgiven, and accepted. Remember how intimate we were. Remember how we trusted Him with everything in childlike faith. Remember how our favorite thing was just being with Him and how we sensed His presence in everything we were doing. Remember when there was nothing to earn, nothing to prove, and no one to impress. Remember when we lived freely in the expanse of His grace.

Paul needed to remember grace. He was trying hard and praying hard to overcome a weakness in his life when Jesus said to him, "My grace is sufficient for you, for power is perfected in weakness" (2 Corinthians 12:9). Paul had forgotten that it was not his strength, but God's grace, that provided sufficiency for living life. This is God's reminder to you as well: "My grace is sufficient for you." It matters not what kind of storm is swirling around you or in you, the reminder is the same: You are God's beloved. He delights in you. Remember . . . Remember. . . .

Repent

The second "invitation" Jesus issues is the cry that opens His ministry, "Repent, for the kingdom of heaven is at hand" (Matthew 3:2). Repent is a word that has lost its force by becoming relegated to religious usage. In the religious world, repentance conjures up notions of deep sorrow, contrition, and radical changes of behavior. These steps may accompany repentance, but they do not constitute it. To repent is simply "to change one's mind."[8] To become a Christian I had to change my mind about God and how I could come to know Him. The initial—and I might add, recurring—repentance of the spiritual life is the movement from earning to receiving, from law to grace, from religion to gospel. This is the repentance to which Jesus calls us.

For me this means living a "gospel life" rather than a "Bible life." I once read an article in a theological journal that asked pastors the question, "Are you preaching the Bible in the light of the gospel, or are you preaching the gospel in the light of the Bible?" To me, the article spoke more about how to live. When I first came to Christ, I came empty handed, eagerly receiving the gospel of grace. The longer I was a Christian the less focused I became on the gracious relationship I had with Christ, and the more intent I was on obeying the commands of the Bible. I was living the gospel in light of the Bible. I had become like the priest and the Levite in the parable of the Good Samaritan who knew how to obey the rules of conduct, but did not comprehend what it meant to love their hurting neighbor.

Some teenagers I know who are committed to Christ are the best reminders to me of the gospel life. They are able to accept, tolerate, and embrace their nonChristian friends with Christ's love in a way that almost seems effortless to me. They are not "straining out gnats" and "swallowing camels," as many of us older Christians are so prone to do. They have given their attention to matters of love, justice, and mercy. They cause me to "change my mind" (repent) in the way Jesus encourages me to. I find myself shedding "elder brother Christianity" and embracing the "prodigal" in myself and in others, as God does.

Changing our mind about what matters most to God—issues of the heart—keeps our soul on the path of grace.

Repeat

The last instruction Jesus gives is, "do the deeds you did at first" (Revelation 2:5)—a call to the actions of obedience.

Early in the Christian life, many of us responded to the grace we received with grateful and loving service to our Lord, expecting nothing in return. But as we grew more aware of how obedient and serving we had become—that is, more self-aware—we may have thought we had earned an extra share of God's blessing.

Compare these two passages — the first of which rebukes the Ephesians, the second of which commends the Thessalonians:

1. Revelation 2:2: I know your deeds and your toil and perseverance.
2. 1 Thessalonians 1:3: . . . constantly bearing in mind your work [deeds] of faith and labor [toil] of love and steadfastness [perserverance] of hope in our Lord Jesus Christ.

Though they have been translated differently, "deeds" and "work" are the same Greek word; "toil" and "labor" are the same word; and "perseverance" and "steadfastness" are the same word. Though the words are identical, one set of actions is rebuked and the other commended. That is because the Thessalonians had not left their first love, nor fallen from grace; because their "work" came from faith, their "labor" was one of love, and their "steadfastness" sprang from their anchoring hope in Christ. Their deeds flowed out of souls that were walking in the light of grace. So their deeds were outward evidence of an inward reality.

ON COURSE

What I have outlined are simple steps that will lead you from the wearying sidetrack of self-effort, self-righteousness, or self-contempt. These steps will lead you back to the path of grace — the place where we find help from the Lifter of our souls.

I recommend that you make a prayer similar to this one your daily cry to God:

Lord Jesus, we are silly sheep who dare to stand before You and try to bribe You with our preposterous portfolios. Suddenly we have come to our senses. We are sorry and ask You to forgive us. Give us the grace to admit we are ragamuffins, to embrace our brokenness, to celebrate Your mercy when we are at our weakest, to rely on Your mercy no matter what we may do. Dear Jesus, gift us to stop grandstanding and trying to get attention, to do the truth quietly without display, to let the dishonesties in our lives fade away, to accept our limitations, to cling to the gospel of grace, and to delight in Your love. Amen.[9]

CHAPTER SIX

HUMILITY: THE
PATH THROUGH SELF

*For thus says the high and exalted One who lives forever,
whose name is Holy, "I dwell on a high and holy place,
and also with the contrite and lowly of spirit in order
to revive the spirit of the lowly."*

ISAIAH 57:15

*A humble understanding of yourself is a surer way to God
than a profound searching after knowledge.*

THOMAS À KEMPIS[1]

He was young, attractive, wealthy, and fun-loving. Excitement and revelry were his pursuits. Fame and success were his dreams. To put it bluntly, he was full of himself.

Then his charmed life was rudely interrupted by discouragement and illness. After two long years of suffering, his soul was awakened to the deeper questions of life and to a search for God. At twenty-five, this spoiled young man responded simply and obediently to God's voice calling him through the gospel. For him that meant renouncing his inheritance and selling his possessions in order to follow Christ in poverty and simplicity. The result of his humility and obedience was the most widespread spiritual awakening in the church in the Middle Ages. "The renewal movement this young man founded was a return to the gospel teachings of Jesus with such force that it shook the entire world."[2]

Francis Bernardone of the small Italian hill town of Assisi had discovered one of the most powerful secrets of the Christian spiritual life—the path of humility and self-emptying. So greatly did the light of Christ shine in him that his very being exerted a powerful attraction on people throughout 13th-century Europe. When asked why the whole world seemed to be running after him, he replied that it was "perhaps because of all men he had the least to boast of in himself."[3] Even on his deathbed he longed to continue to serve his Lord because he felt he had done so little to obey the call of Christ. Such humility was evident in his willing and joyful experience of the presence of God within Him, no matter what was happening to him outwardly.

The dominant note of Francis's life was a joyful selflessness combined with a simple Christlikeness. His transformation from a person who was full of himself into a person full of Christ is captured in a delightful story from *The Little Flowers of St. Francis*. In this account, Francis teaches one of his brothers, Brother Leo, the meaning of perfect joy. As they walked together in the rain and the cold, Francis explained that perfect joy was not in knowledge, wealth, comfort, or success, as many people believed, and as he had once believed.

Frustrated, Brother Leo asked, "I beg you in God's name to tell me where perfect joy is." Francis then itemized a list of the most humiliating and insulting experiences imaginable, adding after each one, "Brother Leo, write that perfect joy is there!" He concluded the matter by saying, "Above all the graces and gifts of the Holy Spirit which Christ gives to His friends is that of conquering oneself, and willingly enduring sufferings, insults, humiliations, and hardships for the love of Christ."[4]

It has been said of Francis's brand of humility that it is "a virtue all preach, none practice, and yet everyone is content to hear." In the twentieth century, it is doubtful that we even want to hear of such humility, much less practice it. A network TV "forum" once considered whether sportsmanship still existed—or whether it should exist in professional sports. A similar forum could be held for the North American church on the subject of humility.

What strikes you, as a modern reader, is that nowhere in Francis's teachings do you find the language of self-fulfillment. Instead we find the spirit of humility and self-effacement. He is truly an ancient voice crying in the modern wilderness of inflated egos, self-importance and promotion, and the exalting of ambition. Others who knew how to keep the soul growing in Christ join with Francis in calling us to this path. Oswald Chambers calls humility "the great characteristic of the [true Christian]." A.W. Tozer writes that, "For the Christian, humility is absolutely indispensable. Without it there can be no self-knowledge, no repentance, no faith, and no salvation."[5]

Today, we experience frustration after frustration as Christians. Things do not go our way and we sulk, wondering what God is up to. Why isn't He answering our prayers? Making life easier? Getting troublesome people sorted out? So we feel weary and want to give up. Or else we feel stuck in a rote faith that has no life to it.

Could it be that our problem is double-mindedness? We want heaven later but we do not want to be conformed to the enormous and loving will of the One who rules heaven. How can this be?

What follows is a distillation of Francis's teaching and spiritual direction. It is meant to lead you out of a frustrating life, in which your will and God's carry on an invisible tug of war, into the path of humility.

THE HEART OF CHRIST—IN YOU

To begin, humility is essential to the Christian spiritual life because receiving God's empowering grace requires me to recognize my need for help. Humility serves as the empty hand that receives God's love and grace. James gives a clear summary of the biblical teaching on the subject: "God is opposed to the proud, but gives grace to the humble." (James 4:6).

You see, I can go quite a way on my own strength if I am living to achieve my own will. No humility is required at all, but I am not living in the directable, teachable, surrendered spirit of Christ. Then again, if, in my self-sufficient, self-determined planning I am going away from God's plan for me—wandering like a sheep gone astray—I am headed out on my own. In fact, God may even try to oppose me, to redirect me into His chosen path for my life.

When I push through life in my own ambitious strength, is the headwind I encounter really God, opposing me in order to wake me up to my need? Or when I have that other kind of pride, the wounded kind that blames God and everyone else for not making my life what I hoped it would be, is it really true that God is the one withholding spiritual blessings of peace from me? If I walk in self-sufficiency, keeping God out of the central place in my soul, I have opposed the One who is the fire of life itself. It is no wonder, then, that I feel confused and wandering in spirit.

On this path, we make the first critical steps into Christlikeness. After the movements of grace, humility is the most important step from self-centeredness to a life centered in God. These movements occur in ever-deepening cycles. It seems now that the earlier steps of submitting career and lifestyle to God were relatively easy compared to the later call to submit to God my dreams for my children, notions of what is best for me and my family, and, finally, to place all of my desires into God's hands. Hearing these calls to humility and responding to them is a necessary aspect of the spiritual journey to union and communion with God in the spirit of Christ.

The path of humility causes me to divest myself until I possess nothing because it has all been placed at God's command. That is why we must be "poor in spirit" to enter the Kingdom. Until then, everything is under our control and very little is under the direction of God. And yet here is the point of amazing spiritual power. For when I am poor in spirit,

I can receive God's grace in full measure and finally experience the truth of Jesus' statement that "theirs is the kingdom of heaven" (Matthew 5:3).

There are no shortcuts to humility. We find no books titled *Humility and How I Achieved It*. In fact, when Bernard of Clairvaux set out to write about the steps to humility, he ended up writing about the steps to pride. When questioned about it he replied, "I can teach only what I have learned."[6] We must follow the slogan of a wise but unknown craftsman who advised, "Don't learn the tricks of the trade, learn the trade." The tricks of the trade of humility would be of the sort that substitute the outer appearance of humility for its reality in the soul. This is a temptation we must resist. The authentic path of humility consists of humbling ourselves before God and before people—no tricks and no shortcuts.

Pride is humanity's titanic self-assertion in the face of God. It is the desire to be like God, the act of a creature usurping the Creator's rightful place. Both Lucifer and Adam fell to this evil desire. This original sin continues as the fundamental, recurring sin of our race. Pride is the attitude that exalts self above God. It is that simple. Pride violates the first commandment, "You shall have no other gods before me." Turning this commandment on its head, pride says, "Love yourself with all your heart, soul, mind, and strength." Pride inflates the self while destroying the soul.

Humility toward God returns me to my proper role as a creature caught in the worship of an awe-inspiring God—a God who loves me and gives Himself for me. I relinquish my arrogant demands to "be like God," to be in charge of my life and instead, like Christ, bend to God in all things. Only Jesus, through His life and teachings, demonstrates most clearly what humility is.

Jesus' Example: Self-Emptying

When Almighty God became human, it was the greatest act of humility that the world has seen, or will ever see. The apostle Paul explains that in becoming human, Jesus let go of His equality with God and "emptied Himself" (Philippians 2:7a). He poured out the divine prerogatives of omniscience, omnipotence, and omnipresence as He took "the form of a bond-servant" (verse 7b). Every word and action of Jesus' earthly life was testimony to His attitude, which was to submit to the leadership of the Father, to demonstrate for us the peace and strength of such a directed life. He did nothing on His own initiative, but did only what He saw the Father doing and taught only what He heard from the Father (John 5:19; 8:28). Jesus said that His food was to do the will of the Father because He did not seek His own will, but the will of the One who sent Him (John 4:34; 5:30). His unswerving obedience to the Father "to the point of death" led him to pray in utter humility on the night before His death, "remove this cup from Me; yet not what I will, but what Thou wilt" (Mark 14:36).

This is humility before God, the surrender of our will to His. This is what Paul had in mind when he wrote, "Have this attitude in yourselves which was also in Christ Jesus" (Philippians 2:5). Upon the axis of humility, one's entire life turns. As C.S. Lewis wrote, "There are only two kinds of people in the end: those who say to God, 'Thy will be done,' and those to whom God says, in the end, 'Thy will be done'."[7] This is what theologian Karl Rahner called everyone's "fundamental option,"[8] being for or against God. Augustine described it as a choice between two "cities." We can choose to live in the City of God, which consists of those who love God to the denial of self, or in the City of the World, inhabited by those who love self above God. Herein is the ultimate difference between humility and pride.

The question each of us must answer is, "Do I want to have in myself the attitude of Christ Jesus?" Jesus declined to be the master of His own fate but continually said to God, "Into Thy hands I commit My spirit." If this is your prayer, you are ready to walk the path of humility before God.

BECOMING AS A CHILD

In Mark, we read that the disciples were keeping the children away from Jesus, much to His displeasure. He sternly told them, "Permit the children to come to Me; . . . for the kingdom of God belongs to such as these. Truly I say to you, whoever does not receive the kingdom of God like a child shall not enter it *at all*" (Mark 10:14-16, emphasis added). What does it mean to become like a child? Jesus gave the answer in Matthew 18:4: "Humble yourself."

Psalm 131 gives a touching picture of the humility of a child when the psalmist writes, "my heart is not proud, or my eyes haughty. . . . Like a weaned child rests against his mother, my soul is like a weaned child within me." The child is not too proud to crawl into his mother's lap and rest. The child is dependent, admitting the need for love, security, and protection. As a result, the child is carefree under the care and guidance of the parent.

Peter Kreeft explains, "If we come to God with empty hands, He will fill them. If we come with full hands, He finds no place to put Himself. It is our beggary, our receptivity, that is our hope."[9] Yet it is the poverty of emptiness that we fear. It is the rare individual who can accept the loss of a job, relationship, or dream as the creation of an empty space in our ambitions that God can now fill. We labor ferociously to keep emptiness from gaining a place in our lives. We hold on tightly to anything that seems to make life work for us, and we lose our soul in trying to make permanent a world that is changing beneath our feet every day. And so we fail to enter in spirit into the Kingdom where God's great plan for us is ongoing.

Either we embrace our poverty of spirit, or we live a life of anxiety. It is when I accept my poverty that a heavenly "blessedness" rushes in; when I admit my thirst that the water of life refreshes me. And when I face the darkness of my own void, the light of Christ has a chance to illuminate my soul.

For when I am willing to let go of my life, Jesus gives me His.

A SERVANT TO ALL

The apostle Peter observes that the "genuineness" of our faith is proved in our response to trials. Likewise, the proof that we have taken our place under God is seen by the way we respond in our everyday relationships.

The apostle John asks: How can a person love God whom he can't see, if he doesn't love his brother whom he can see? (1 John 4:20). If I really want to know the condition of my heart, I need only look at my relationships—especially with people who rub me the wrong way or who flatter me to get in my favor.

Here are five questions to ask yourself, if you want to begin to follow God on the path of humility.

1. Am I willing to see myself as a servant of all? (See Mark 10:42-45)

Servanthood is both the thermometer and the thermostat of humility. The extent of my willingness to be a servant reveals the extent of my humility. Conversely, there is no better way to deepen humility than by choosing to be a servant. Richard Foster, in *Celebration of Discipline*, wisely makes the distinction between "choosing to serve and choosing to be a servant."[10] Choosing to serve allows me to stay comfortably in charge. I decide when, where, and whom I will serve. This kind of service can actually produce pride rather than humility, as the focus remains on what is good for me. On the other hand, when I choose to be a servant of God, I have placed myself "on call" to God as He directs me in serving others.

I once served a two-year stint as chaplain in a homeless shelter. Each day, I would show up to work having no idea what lay ahead. I was simply there to serve whomever entered the door. One day it was a single mother needing rent money to keep from getting evicted that afternoon. Later, a runaway teenager asked for help in buying a bus ticket home. Next, an elderly homeless man simply needed someone to listen to his story. Every person was unique in personality and situation, but as I learned over time, every one was very much alike in needing someone to care.

2. Am I willing to associate with those I naturally think of as "lower"? (See Romans 12:16)

The humility of Jesus led Him to become the friend of tax-gatherers and sinners, as well as prostitutes, thieves, and other outcasts. Jesus moved toward the poor and the powerless. He practiced downward mobility. He gravitated toward those who desperately needed Him. In light of this attribute of Jesus, we might ask ourselves, "Who are my friends?"

James states that "if you show partiality, you are committing sin" (James 2:9). He was speaking about a real situation in which Christians were showing partiality based on the appearance of wealth. One person came to church dressed in fine clothes and jewelry and was given a seat of honor. A poor person came in and was told to stand in the back. The apostle said that showing this kind of "personal favoritism" arises out of "evil motives" (verses 1-4).

While I was in seminary, one of my professors called attention to our institution's preferential treatment of the rich and powerful by giving them a seat on the platform during chapel. He observed that other guests had to find a seat on their own and were generally ignored. Both personally and corporately we must examine our motives and practices in this regard if we are serious about being clothed in humility toward one another (1 Peter 5:5).

3. Am I willing to let God transform my focus until I consider others before I consider myself? (See Philippians 2:3)

We do not need to think less *of* ourselves, but we do need to think less *about* ourselves. A self-centered life is not a Christian life.

Once I met a young man with cerebral palsy who incarnated this truth to me. I was on the staff of a Young Life camp in the mountains of Colorado, and Steve was on the work crew. The rugged terrain made it very difficult for him to get around, yet I never heard him complain and he always greeted me with a smile. One guy on staff had been troubled by a toothache and made no secret of it for several days. After he returned from the dentist, Steve approached him with sincere concern, asking about the tooth. The other guy was stopped in his tracks. He realized that a minor toothache had caused him to be totally self-centered, while Steve, with a lifelong debilitating illness, was free to consider the toothache more important than his daily struggles with cerebral palsy.

4. Am I willing to take the lower place? (See Luke 14:7-11)

In one parable, Jesus tells of dinner guests who are vying for the best places at the table. The conclusion, in Jesus' words, is this: "everyone who exalts himself shall be humbled, and he who humbles himself shall be exalted." Peter, in his first letter, adds that God will exalt the humble "at the proper time." This is what makes taking the lower place so challenging. It may be a long time before I am asked to "move up higher."

The following story about Senator Mark Hatfield, who displayed Christ in the self-promoting world of politics, encourages me to take the lower place. He attended a weekly Bible study luncheon at his church in Washington along with many other politicians and busy professionals. When the meeting was over, almost everyone would rush out to get back to their "important business." But Senator Hatfield would often be seen folding and stacking chairs after everyone else had left. The pastor commented that no one in attendance bore the magnitude of responsibilities that Senator Hatfield carried. Nonetheless, he chose to stay to do the menial task, much as Jesus did by taking up the towel and the basin at the Last Supper and washing the disciples' feet. When He had finished, Jesus called us all to the lower place: "For I gave you an example that you also should do as I did to you" (John 13:15).

The secret of Jesus' service, and of ours, is to offer all of our selves to God, and God alone.

5. Am I willing to allow God to change my heart so that I respond more humbly to praise and criticism? (See 2 Samuel 23:13-17)

What I crave is the praise, adulation, and admiration of anyone who will offer it, loving to be exalted, rather than being humble before the Lord. Those in positions of Christian leadership would do well to consider and follow David's example of deflecting praise and devotion to our Lord, who alone is worthy to receive it.

David demonstrated humility, even toward someone who was treating him unjustly. On several occasions during the time Saul was trying to kill him, David had the opportunity to do away with Saul. He refused, saying he would not lift his hand against the Lord's anointed. Jesus said that we are to love our enemies and pray for those who persecute us (Matthew 5:44). Paul's interpretation is simply, "Never pay back evil for evil to anyone" (Romans 12:17).

Is this my response to those who advocate political causes I consider immoral and unbiblical? Do I pray for those who criticize me? Am I an agent of Christ's love to those I disagree with? Or do I take the easy path and love only those who love me? The acid test of my humility is how I respond when I am criticized, opposed, or persecuted. Jesus prayed for forgiveness for those who crucified Him, and we are called to follow in His steps.

IS THIS EVEN POSSIBLE?

How could I ever walk before God at that level? Thomas à Kempis helps us find the source of power to enter on that pathway. *The Imitation of Christ* is a classic statement of Christian humility, and its wisdom reflects the central concern for those who desire to walk in humility:

> Prop yourself up with and for Christ if you wish to live with Christ. If just once you could perfectly enter the inner life of Jesus and experience a little of His passionate love, then you would not care at all about what you might gain or lose in life. You would even bear insults gladly, for the love of Jesus makes a person think of himself in a very humble way.[11]

If you have gotten stuck in the flatness of self, the path of humility will change its very landscape. For when you walk this path your soul will encounter the dramatic contours of the living presence of Christ. And you will find your inner person coming alive, perhaps as never before.

Isn't that what you've been thirsting for?

CHAPTER SEVEN

PRAYING THE PSALMS: THE PATH THROUGH SHALLOWNESS

Out of the depths I cried to Thee, O LORD.
PSALM 130:1

[Crying to God from the depths] is how most Christians for most of the Christian centuries have matured in prayer.
EUGENE PETERSON[1]

I t was a time of grief—and they had lost confidence in God's ability to help. Joe and Francis's daughter, Heather, was diagnosed in June with a rare disease that in November proved to be fatal. Their lives were in a downward spiral for the two years that followed. They could not relate to the praise songs or upbeat testimonies they heard in church.

God seemed completely absent, except for one small brush of contact that came from Psalm 137:

> By the rivers of Babylon we sat and wept when we remembered Zion . . . our captors asked us for songs, our tormentors demanded songs of joy; they said, "Sing us one of the songs of Zion!" How can we sing the songs of the LORD while in a foreign land? (verses 1-4, NIV)

The psalm provided the only words for prayer as they wandered in the foreign land of grief. It became their Bible study, their song, and their prayer. These lines somehow kept them going, because they spoke from the depths of Joe and Francis's soul.

THE DESIRES OF OUR HEART

"Please, Lord, help my child [or spouse, or friend]." "Bless these efforts, Lord." "Just give me what I'm asking for, and I'll do whatever You want."

Many of us have been taught that prayer is "simply asking." Others have learned "patterns" to pray by, such as that provided by "acrostics" similar to ACTS: Adoration, Confession, Thanksgiving, Supplication. But after a while, what has passed for prayer—our soul's conversation with God—can seem flat and incomplete. Some complain that praying,

98

in their experience, is like a bird flitting from branch to branch, without ever feeling that they are "lighting" or getting a good grip on anything substantial.

Prayer becomes listless, bland, and meaningless from time to time. Most often, this is because we stay on the shallow level of our wants or believe we must pray in some formulaic pattern.

For those who have experienced pain or loss, like Joe and Francis, prayer seems daunting. It is hard to face God with the frustration, disappointment, and anger that comes when—though we have prayed—someone we dearly love suffers or dies, or something we deeply want is denied. How can we be that honest with a holy God—One who also has the eternal verdict over our soul?

I would venture to say that most Christians to whom I've offered direction have not learned how to enter a deep heart-relationship with God by following the path of wholehearted prayer that comes from the roots of their being. For many, to learn this requires a change in our understanding of prayer and a change in our willingness to pray.

Learning prayer as "soul conversation" depends on our willingness to participate in two realities: first, developing an awareness of the depth of our own life experiences; second, establishing a willingness to listen to what God may be trying to say to us out of the depths of His heart.

This is where the psalmists can provide spiritual direction for us. They safely guide our souls beyond the boundaries of the life we have pictured for ourselves, out to touch the infinite. It is there that our soul can have a true encounter with God—perhaps for the first time.

OUT OF THE SHALLOWS

The first step in praying from the heart is to face and know our own emotions. It does little good to smile politely to God and say the "right" things when inside we are blistering with anger. In failing to connect with our own heart, we live with shallow, superficial relationships with others—including God. My first task, then, and yours, is to get at the deep roots of emotion buried in us.

This task is critical because our emotions are connected to our dreams, visions, goals, and plans—our will for our lives. When these are crossed or denied, our feelings begin to churn. Sometimes life trains us, in various ways, to ignore, cover, or deny what we feel. And so a denied dream is buried beneath a layer of denied or ignored emotion. We tell ourselves, "I shouldn't want this in the first place." Or "I should not feel this way." But we do want, and we do feel. And these wants and feelings drive us.

If we resist our soul, our true self, long enough, we lose awareness of the drives and emotions hidden inside. When you and I feel anger or sadness, for instance, but we are unwilling or unable to look inside at its source in us, these powerful emotions will fester and corrupt the inner person. This will also be true of our unwillingness to examine the source of fear, anxiety, depression, despair, or our compulsions.

Since prayer is the soul's conversation with God, is it any wonder that when I am out of touch with my inner world I feel dry, blocked, or dead in my prayer life?

A personal journal entry from several years ago reveals the frustration that led me to the psalms:

> During the last year I have been drawn to the psalms because
> of the intensity and honesty of the struggles they portray in a
> person's relationship to God and the world. For years the
> verse about not knowing how to pray as I ought served as an
> excuse for my sophomoric efforts in conversation with God,
> when in reality God Himself had supplied a toolbox for con-
> structing a meaningful prayer life. All of the formulas, acros-
> tics, and gimmicks to make praying simple and easy are
> exposed as shallow in the face of the pulsating reality, life,
> and depth of the psalms as a guide to prayer. I learn to pray
> by praying, and the psalms provide the pattern for me. As I
> pray the psalms, they leave their mark on my soul until finally
> I find my own prayers conforming to the original pattern.

Only later did I learn that my experience with the psalms was part of a long and deep tradition within the church that has been shared by millions, as one commentator observes:

> The psalms have been used widely and continuously to nur-
> ture and guide personal meditations and devotions. Christians
> have said them as their own prayers, as guides to learning to

pray, and as texts through which they came to know themselves and God more surely.[2]

WORKOUT FOR SPIRITUAL FITNESS

The fourth century bishop, Ambrose of Milan, mentor to Augustine, called the psalms "a gymnasium of the soul."[3] Trying to pray when you are out of touch with your soul is like trying to compete in a wrestling match without physical conditioning. God wants us to put muscle in our prayer so that He can have a real and vigorous encounter with us.

Explore the path of praying through psalms, and I believe you will be irresistibly drawn to this marvelous book of the Bible as your lifetime prayer guide, as countless Christians through the ages have been.

RAW HONESTY IN PRAYER GIVES LIFE TO THE SOUL

Some time ago, in a time of dryness, I was a bit startled when the following scripture leaped out at me one morning, as if I had written it myself:

> Why, God, do you turn a deaf ear? Why do you make your-
> self scarce? (Psalm 88:14, MSG)

After some weeks of praying the psalms, dramatic changes began to occur in my relationship with God as this journal entry indicates:

> The joyous result for me has been freedom to pray the full
> range of my feelings, whether positive or negative, without
> having my feelings dictating my response to God. I feel I
> have been given permission to be nakedly honest with myself
> and before the Lord. Now I know from experience that God is
> fully able to handle my honest, gut-level responses to the raw
> edge of life as I struggle before Him. It is a tremendous com-
> fort to realize that honesty does not mean infidelity, but that
> honesty is a prerequisite to fidelity.

I understood John Calvin's observation that "the psalms are an anatomy of all the parts of the soul."[4] There is no emotion that is not brought to the encounter with God—including those we consider negative, such as anger, hate, fear, or bitterness. In the safe presence of a merciful God, we are free to express any feeling—even if we feel betrayed or abandoned by God.

Even Jesus, the author and perfecter of our faith, cried out from the depths of His being many times. Most memorably, He shouted in terrible pain from the cross, in words from the psalms, "My God, my God, why hast Thou forsaken me?" (Psalm 22:1). As the very life within Him was failing, He breathed, "Into your hands I commit my spirit" (Psalm 31:5, NIV). At no time did Jesus "pretend" in prayer, or cover His soul's deepest cry. He prayed out of despair, confusion, excruciating anxiety, and betrayal by friends.

Strangely, out of the crucible of honest prayer, amazing transformation occurs.

Speak honestly with God, as Jesus did, in real human joy and agony. You will begin to see that when we come to the end of our emotions, we are given strength of soul to make the most powerful step we can ever make—a step toward binding our whole being to the mighty will of God. We are given strength by the Holy Spirit to honestly pray Jesus' prayer: "Father, into Thy hands I commit My spirit" (Luke 23:46).

Out of the various fears or mild despairs of midlife, knowing that fundamental things like health are out of my control, and that the chance for achieving certain things with my life is gone, I have, for instance, felt the sting of the psalmist's words while praying: "I am forgotten as a dead man, out of mind, I am like a broken vessel" (Psalm 31:12). At times, I did not know the despair was in me until the words found it out. And as I continued, the psalmist brought me from despair to something new, as I continued to pray in his words, knowing that despite my timetable of life, "my times are in Thy hand" (verse 15) and "great is Thy goodness" (verse 19). As I take these truths deep into my soul, to confront my human dismay, I find that my dismal spirit is lifted and changed, and I am led to acknowledge that though life is passing quickly, I am ultimately safe "in the secret place of [God's] presence" (verse 20).

GIVING VOICE TO THE WHOLE INNER PERSON

Many Christians I encounter are, as I mentioned earlier, afraid to "bring up" certain matters to God because they might move out of God's grace or presence. David had no such fear, for he saw the truth: "Where can I go from Thy Spirit? Or where can I flee from Thy presence?" (Psalm 139:7).

Many of the methods that instruct us in prayer are "polite ways" to address God. In certain traditions, prayer books help Christians learn how to address God and to understand something of His ways. Yet Scripture indicates that God wants to know all that is in us. Formula prayers may exclude part of me or what I am experiencing.

The call of the Bible is not to offer more prayers, but to have a life of unceasing prayer, as the apostle Paul expresses in 1 Thessalonians 5:17. That means to have a life that flows out in true conversation of the soul so that we are "abiding," as Jesus put it, with our true self open to God. The psalms are the only prayer guide that enlarges prayer so that everything is pulled into it. Nothing is left out.

Martin Luther spoke of the psalms pathway like this:

> The Psalter is the book of all saints; and everyone, in whatever situation he may be, finds in that situation psalms and words that fit his case, that suit him as if they were put there just for his sake, so that he could not put it better himself, or find or wish for anything better.[5]

THE PRAYER OF GOD'S HEART

Obviously, there is a time when I must turn from my own soul-contents to concerns beyond myself. It is important to pray for the concerns that are on the heart of God.

In many psalms we encounter God's concern for all the nations and for affairs that lie beyond our everyday worlds. On my own, I would pray only about my own self-serving concerns. Allowing God to direct the focus of our heart onto His concerns is another key in allowing the character of Christ to be formed in me. The psalms lead me, for instance, to remember the poor, and to take God's heart into my own, for He "raises the poor from the dust, and lifts the needy from the ash heap" (Psalm 113:7). I understand that He not only sees the afflicted, but that He will act on their behalf—perhaps commissioning me to somehow help in this work.

As you see, the psalmists eventually redirect our focus toward God: "My soul *waits* in silence for God only . . . He only is my rock and my salvation" (Psalm 62:1-2, emphasis added).

Though God invites us to know our hearts, we are not meant to stay stuck there. For many, ongoing struggles are the result of self-absorption. Some time ago, I experienced a "deliverance" from self-centered praying, as a journal entry chronicles:

> Finally, I see that sincere praise is the final destination of the journey of prayer though there may be several short stops along the way. This is the true work of prayer: to respond honestly to Jesus, the Word, circumstances, and relationships before the Lord so that the end result is the ability to worship in spirit and truth.

And so, though psalm-praying often begins with the human agenda, it moves beyond to open the heart of God to us—to let us internalize His response to human need. What we discover then is a great heart of compassion—God's heart beating within our own.

What else would our ultimate response be to the fantastic discovery of encountering God's heart in us? With few exceptions, most psalms end with bursts of praise.

In fact, the Hebrew title for the Book of Psalms is "Praises." The goal of praying the psalms is to lead us into the deepest part of our being, where our true selves exist, and then to open the door of the soul so we can move out beyond ourselves into the majesty and glory of almighty God. The fourth century bishop, Athanasius, understood that the psalms not only stir up the emotions but also moderate them—that is, they give godly shape and direction to our otherwise wild-growing feelings. The end movement of the soul is praise.

Ultimately, the psalms shift the center of my spiritual gravity, as Peterson points out:

> The psalms were not prayed by people trying to understand themselves. They are not the record of people searching for the meaning of life. They were prayed by people who understood that God had everything to do with them. God, not their feelings, was the center. God, not their souls, was the issue. God, not the meaning of life, was critical.[6]

I move out of myself and into God when praying a psalm such as this: "Thou art my LORD; I have no good besides Thee. . . . Thou wilt make known to me the path of life; In Thy presence is fulness of joy; In Thy right hand there are pleasures forever" (Psalm 16:2,11).

C.S. Lewis, in his book *Reflections on the Psalms*, likewise refers to praying the psalms as an experience that is fully God-centered.[7] Speaking the words of the Spirit-directed prayers, I find that even my concerns, whether petty or important, are leading me to God. I discover that in the midst of the chaos that is my life, God is creating, saving, and redeeming. I learn to stop feeling ashamed, angry, confused, or disappointed about this process, and I begin to praise Him for it.

THE PSALMS TEACH US TO RESPOND TO GOD AND HIS WORK IN THE WORLD

Prayer is the elemental language of response, for God's initiatives require an answer. The psalms provide us with 150 "responses" to this God we are coming to know as He moves within our living soul.

In A.W. Tozer's book *The Pursuit of God*, he assures us that we can stand firm upon three facts about the One to whom we pray: God is previous, God is present now, and God is speaking.[8] Therefore, the first word is God's, but the response that brings health to our soul must come from us.

For instance, God has spoken to us first in creation, and we bring health to our soul when we respond in psalms of praise: "O LORD, our Lord, How majestic is Thy name in all the earth" (Psalm 8:1). God has spoken in salvation, for which we have psalms of thanksgiving: "What shall I render to the LORD for all His benefits toward me? . . .To Thee I shall offer a sacrifice of thanksgiving" (Psalm 116:12,17). God has spoken through our circumstances and the psalms of lament give voice to our soul: "Evening and morning and at noon, I will complain and murmur, and He will hear my voice" (Psalm 55:17). God speaks even through injustice, and our soul's response is shaped by the "imprecatory" psalms (those that ask God to judge evil): "Rise up, O Judge of the earth; render recompense to the proud" (Psalm 94:2). God speaks through our consciences so we are furnished with soul-prayers of confession: "I know my transgressions, and my sin is ever before me" (Psalm 51:3).

Do you see what is happening here? God is speaking to us, showing us that He is on the move everywhere in the world—even in situations where we are tempted to believe He is absent. He is opening our minds to His presence and work in all things.

In this way, praying the psalms sharpens our spiritual senses. Our soul learns to listen attentively for God's presence and voice in the world, in others, in the Word, in ourselves, and in our present circumstances. And the psalms give us a vocabulary with which to respond to God and His movements in the real world.

THE PSALMS BOND OUR SOUL TO THE COMMUNITY OF FAITH

When we allow our soul to be directed by the psalms, we are not entering the solitude of the prayer closet. We find ourselves in the company of fellow worshipers gathered in God's sanctuary. The Psalter was the prayer book for the temple and synagogue from David's time onward. Praying the psalms we do not pray alone, but our soul begins to bond with others in this vast, timeless community of believers.

A preposition is the part of speech that governs relationships between words. Psalms teach us the proper "prepositions of prayer"; that is, the relationships that happen in prayer. So the prepositions that are attached to the noun "prayer" tell us the kind of praying that is being offered. And so we find that the psalms direct us to "pray with," "pray under," and to "pray for."

For the healthy growth of the soul, we need to understand what each of these types of psalm-praying means.

Prayer With . . .

All the prayers in the psalms are prayed with others. We know this from the liturgical markers inserted throughout the Book of Psalms. Seventy-one times we see the Hebrew word *selah* as a notation in the margin. Scholars can only guess at its exact meaning, but what is certain is that it indicates a direction for group worship.

Praying and singing the psalms together would have been the practice of Jesus and His disciples as they observed the Jewish tradition of morning and evening prayer. Paul encouraged the Christians to use the psalms in their community worship (see Ephesians 5:19, Colossians 3:16). Hughes Old, a scholar of Christian worship and liturgy, says definitively, "Praying the psalms together has long been one of the most cherished traditions of Christian worship."[9]

Today, we feel restless if worship does not move us as individuals. Worship is meant to be centered upon God. And it is also an act that binds me to a community, rather than dividing me from others who do not desire the form or emotional pitch of worship that I prefer.

Jesus confirmed this communal nature of worshipful prayer when He said, "For where two or three are gathered together in my name, there am I in the midst of them" (Matthew 18:20, KJV). Therefore, whether alone or in public worship, whenever we pray the psalms we join in prayer with a "great cloud of witnesses" that includes the ancient worshipers of Israel, Jesus and the disciples, the early church, and Christians from two millennia.

If I take the path of psalm-praying, my vision of prayer changes. I am likely to move out of the narrowness of my individualism, and move into participation with the community of faith which is beyond my own personal desires and purposes.

Prayer Under . . .

Not only do we join others when we pray, but the psalms show us that we pray under the direction of someone assigned to lead us in prayer. "To the choir director"—another liturgical direction—occurs as a heading in fifty-five psalms. These psalms show us that a worship leader was commonly a part of the praying life of Israel. The Israelites learned to pray by being led in prayer.

When I am led in prayer, I am freed from the burden of taking the initiative of being in charge, of choosing the right words. I can follow. I can submit. My ego is set aside. Grace rushes in. This was my experience for an entire week that I spent at St. Meinrad Archabbey in Indiana, with 150 Benedictine monks. Three times a day, I joined them for worship and experienced being led in prayer. Praying and singing the psalms together under the direction of the choirmaster were at the heart of the worship. I would often enter the sanctuary full of myself but, after being led in prayer, would leave full of God. Prayer "under" had done its work.

Prayer For . . .

When we take our proper place as part of a praying community, we cannot help but pray "for" those we pray with. This is especially true as we pray the psalms. The psalm that I am praying may be a lament, but I find myself in a "hallelujah mood." Then I become aware of the woman in the next pew who is suffering from cancer or of the brother in the next continent facing starvation. Then I can pray that lament for my brother or sister in pain. Joining our hearts in prayer is a foundation of spiritual community.

JUST DO IT

Some months ago, I encouraged a friend to pursue the soul-path of the psalms. This is a man who has been to seminary, who has been faithfully serving Christ, and who has been seeking the Lord for many years. Recently, he told me, "More than anything else in thirty years of being a Christian, praying the psalms has transformed my relationship with God." For him, it was the simplicity of praying the psalms that made the difference.

There is no "secret" or "key" to praying the psalms. We simply open our Bibles to the book of Psalms and begin. The traditional practice is to divide the psalms into thirty equal segments, one for each day of the month, and pray them. Daily. Sequentially. Simply let the words of the psalms be your prayer. You will begin to notice the connections with your life. You may want to write down what emerges for you as you pray.

I encourage you to follow this path of growth in Christ. Take the psalms into your soul, let them speak to you and for you. Let them move you through the depths, out into new and open spaces. Let them enlarge your soul and lift you beyond yourself, into the fellowship of others who are walking this path in spirit with you—and into the fellowship and praise of God.

CHAPTER EIGHT

GOSPEL MEDITATION: THE PATH THROUGH APATHY

. . . we heard it with our own ears, saw it with our own eyes, verified it with our own hands. The Word of Life appeared right before our eyes; we saw it happen! . . . We saw it, we heard it, and now we're telling you so you can experience it along with us, this experience of communion with the Father and his Son, Jesus Christ.

1 JOHN 1:1,3 MSG

Gary understood why some of the guys at the office were buying new sports cars, escaping into their hobbies, and having affairs. They were all in the same midlife boat. Not one of them had made it to "the top," none was a millionaire, and none had that "perfect" family.

Even his friends in the morning Bible study struggled with boredom, apathy, and lack of purpose. When Gary was honest, he had to admit his faith had become a tiresome "going through the motions." When it came to some things—knowing a sure direction in life, for instance—were he and his friends that much different from the guys at the office? What could bring a passion for living back to his soul?

Many Christians sense that the focus, drive, and vision Jesus had—His sense of purpose in being—is supposed to be part of their experience too. Aren't we supposed to be centered and empowered in a clear vision of God's love and plan, as Christ was? Yet somehow we find ourselves more often wandering at the margins—keeping one eye on God and another scouting the landscape for a more exciting offer. We drift into halfheartedness and boredom, losing our passionate center.

Arctic explorers had a way to keep from becoming lost in a snowstorm. If a companion was missing, they would drive a stake into the snow, tie a long rope to the stake, and then move out in concentric circles until the missing person was found. Similarly, we need to keep our soul anchored—or "staked," as it were—in God, to fix our eyes upon Him as the center point of our spiritual vision. When we learn to move from this center, we stop wandering restlessly at the margins.

The path of gospel meditation has been used for centuries as the "rope" by which we remain tied to the central vision, which is God and His work. It is meditation that opens the "eyes" of the soul, so to speak, so that our inner man begins to perceive God and His ways. And so, the dimension of the invisible starts to become, in a sense, visible to us.

LIVING IN UNREALITY

In the midst of sixteen years of busy ministry my soul lost its proper focus and drifted. Oswald Chambers calls this sliding into "unconscious unreality."[1] That means I was telling people about Jesus, teaching about Jesus, and watching people come to Jesus, but I was not experiencing Jesus myself. He was no longer a real person or a felt presence in my life. I was unaware, unconscious, of this absence of reality. What I was conscious of, however, was a gnawing emptiness and a yearning for something more. But what? I wasn't sure.

Subsequently, I have heard many others who describe themselves as "going through the motions" of their faith. They feel apathy toward God and spiritual things. As one man put it, with a shrug of boredom, "I see no evidence of God in my life."

What we need is to rekindle the kind of longing expressed by John of the Cross, a passionate disciple of Christ, some four centuries ago:

I no longer want just to hear about you, beloved Lord, through messengers. I no longer want to hear doctrines about you, nor to have my emotions stirred by people speaking of you. I yearn for your presence.[2]

There comes a time in our spiritual growth when nothing will satisfy but a real encounter with the indwelling Christ.

OUR PROBLEM

Midway through the twentieth century, A.W. Tozer diagnosed our predicament:

For millions of Christians, nevertheless, God is no more real than He is to the nonChristian. They go through life trying to love an ideal and be loyal to a mere principle.[3]

Today, the gap between what Christians say they believe and what they actually experience has widened precipitously. The quest for the reality of God has lured the church into politics, marketing, entertainment, emotionalism, sensationalism, and any number of other "isms."

We have looked for Jesus in all the wrong places. Elijah did not find God in the whirlwind, or the earthquake, or the fire, but in the "still, small voice." Neither will we find Christ in the noisy or the spectacular until we can first see Him in the quiet and the ordinary—in the reality of our own lives.

This reality is unknowingly missed as our lives become hurried and distracted. One can study and know scores of recipes for bread yet never taste the end result of the recipe. Or a baker can produce loaves of bread in large quantities and never eat one slice. The Bread of Life invites us to take Him deeply into our souls. It is not enough to know all about the Bread or even to deliver the Bread to others. In John 6:26-40, Jesus says that life comes when we eat this living bread. Nothing short of this direct experience of the reality of Christ will satisfy the hunger of our souls.

THE WORD BECAME FRESH

The action of eating is joined with the Word of God when the prophet is fed a scroll filled with God's words (see Ezekiel 3). The prophet finds it is "sweet as honey" in his mouth. He was then to go speak these words to the house of Israel. The metaphor, it is explained, is a figure for taking God's words into the heart (verse 10). They were not to pass through his mind directly to his mouth. Ezekiel was first to be nourished by the Word of God before he proclaimed it to others. It was to be internalized as personal reality for him before it became a public proclamation to others.

Ezekiel provides a picture of the path of gospel meditation. On this path we encounter the living Jesus through the Scriptures. We allow images of His life, actions, and encounters, and teachings to travel the twelve inches from our heads to our hearts. Then we are nourished as Ezekiel was. In time we may find ourselves exclaiming with the disciples on the Emmaus road, "Were not our hearts burning within us while He was speaking to us on the road, while He was explaining the Scriptures to us?" (Luke 24:32).

Do we understand what it means to have the word of God enter our soul like honey, or like bread?

In the New Testament, two terms are used for the "word" of God— *logos* and *rhema*.[4] *Logos* is the large concept that is used most frequently to refer to the word of God in Scripture, as well as to Jesus, the "word" made flesh. The Bible as a whole could be called the *logos* of God. Within this large word of God, there is the *rhema* of God, the "individual words and utterances" that are spoken and personal. *Rhema* is used in Matthew 4 where Jesus declares that man does not live by bread alone, but by every "word"—every utterance spoken to the heart of the individual—that comes from the mouth of God. This is the word that provides nourishment for the soul. Jesus says, "The [*rhemata*] that I have spoken to you are spirit and are life" (John 6:63). Jesus does not say, "The words I speak are spirit and are life." As I hear the words of Jesus spoken directly to me, they become spirit and life. They become food for my soul, the bread of life. The large *logos* becomes the personal *rhema*, the word within the Word.

One such personal word came to me when my soul was nearly dead from serving Christ without knowing the reality of His presence. I read Jesus' declaration, "No longer do I call you slaves . . . but I have called you friends" (John 15:15). Of course I had read, studied, taught, and preached this passage many times, but I had never heard it as a personal word to me. To paraphrase George Fox, founder of the Society of Friends, I did not "possess what I professed." When my soul was well-cultivated— that is, wide open and desperately hungry—the word came to me in a new way and my soul took it in. My image of God and my image of myself were transformed. Up to then I had pictured my relationship to God one-dimensionally as a servant to a master. God was someone to work for and to please. If I did, then I would be blessed. But hearing Jesus call me His friend gave me a new identity and a fresh experience of the love of God. His words were truly spirit and life to my soul.

That experience of *logos* becoming *rhema* was a dramatic one, but this work of the Spirit is actually frequent and commonplace. Many times, after hearing a sermon or reading a Scripture, I have been in a discussion with friends who heard something entirely different from the same word of God. The message we heard was identical—but the word that was heard was unique to each hearer. What greater witness is there that the Holy Spirit takes the Word of God and applies it personally to each heart that is open? When this happens we encounter God directly and person- ally. The Word becomes fresh and real, alive and powerful.

DIRECT ENCOUNTER

Mark Twain commented that he once knew a man who grabbed a cat by the tail and learned 40 percent more about cats than the man who didn't.

Real knowing comes through direct encounter. What is true of cats is more true of people. Why else is a blind date such a fearful event? Though I met my wife Janis on one, a date with an unknown person is generally an experience we approach with great apprehension. Secondhand information, no matter how reliable the source, is no substitute for firsthand experience—yet how much of our knowledge about God is based on someone else's experience, study, or prayer?

For many years I had very little "hands-on" experience with God. I heard and believed what other people said about God but had minimal experience of God myself. For example, a preacher I respected might say, "God is good," and I would believe his word without ever asking myself if I was tasting God's goodness in my own life. I needed to know that goodness in my life.

One of the outstanding theologians of this century, Hans Urs von Balthasar, blazes the trail for the path of gospel meditation.

> We do not understand that once God's word has rung out in
> the midst of the world, in the fullness of time, it is so powerful
> that it applies to everyone, all with equal directness; no one is
> disadvantaged by distance in space or time. . . . To be sure
> Jesus addresses a particular Samaritan woman at the well, but,
> at the same time, in her, he also addresses every sinner,
> woman or man. When Jesus sits, tired, at the well's edge, it is
> not for this one person alone. Therefore it is not a mere "pious
> exercise" when, in spirit, I put myself beside this woman and
> enter into her role. Not only may I play this part; I must play
> it, for I have long been involved in this dialogue without being
> consulted. I am this dried-up soul. . . . So it is not at all enough
> to see the dialogues and encounters presented in the gospel as
> mere "examples," . . . In addressing this repentant sinner he
> addresses every sinner; in speaking to this woman listening at
> his feet he is speaking to every listener. Since it is God who is
> speaking, there can be no historical distance from his word;
> hence, too, our attitude to it cannot be merely historical.
> Instead there is that utter directness which confronted those
> who met him on the roads of Palestine: "Follow me!", "Go
> and sin no more!", "Peace be with you!"[5]

Through gospel meditation we hear the words of Jesus with "utter directness." *Logos* becomes *rhema*. Historical distance vanishes. The word is alive, powerful, personal. When the reality of Jesus is experienced in this way we find ourselves joining with Thomas à Kempis in saying, "Let it, then, be our chief study to meditate on the life of Christ."[6] It is this direct encounter that sparked the fire of devotion for the great saints of the past. By learning from them we can light our candle from their flame.

DIRECTIVES FROM THE SAINTS

Let's consider some of the pathways of gospel meditation, as prescribed by some of history's great spiritual directors.

Ignatius's "Application of the Senses"

Ignatius's famous guide to prayer, *The Spiritual Exercises*, is a series of meditations on the life of Christ that has been widely used for almost five hundred years by those seeking a deeper relationship with their Lord. Ignatius suggests, as a practical aid for gospel meditation, what he called "application," or use of the senses. Whatever story or passage is the focus of your meditation, Ignatius suggests you hear, see, smell, taste, and feel every aspect of it that you can.

For instance, read the passage about the disciples being caught in a storm on the Sea of Galilee. Quietly enter into prayerful meditation, and hear the waves crashing against your boat, feel the wind in your face, smell the fishy odor of the nets in the boat, and see Jesus asleep in the midst of it all. As the scene becomes more alive, Jesus becomes more real.

You may find your heart racing and feel the settled calm that falls when Jesus takes command and says, "Peace, be still."

Francis de Sales' *Discipline of the Mind*

This sort of meditation puts our imaginations into a biblical framework and focuses our thoughts and attention on the ways God penetrates and invades earthly realities. Francis de Sales, in the seventeenth century, explained how this works:

> By means of the imagination we confine our mind within the mystery on which we meditate, that it may not ramble to and

fro, just as we shut up a bird in a cage or tie a hawk by his
leash so that he may rest on the hand.[7]

He uses the term "mystery" as a term of reverence, expressing the
awe we might feel if we keep in mind that God invaded time and space.
And so each event in Jesus' life has a holy mystery to it that must be
plumbed, which we do by opening our souls wide in meditation. This
requires discipline. And the biblical story serves as a "leash" for our minds
to curtail the wandering of our attention, which is a common struggle in
prayer. With our minds confined to the scripture at hand we make it possible for the "word of Christ [to] richly dwell" within us (Colossians 3:16).

Sometimes that word can be a seemingly innocuous question, such
as the one that Jesus asked blind Bartimaeus, "What do you want Me to
do for you?" (Mark 10:51). As I paused with this question in prayerful
meditation, many of my hidden hopes, desires, and dreams came gush-
ing forth. This one question unlocked treasures that had been stored away
for years in my soul. How powerful and gracious is the word of Christ,
even His humble questions!

Alexander Whyte's "Sacred" Imagination

In meditative prayer we seek to live the experience of Scripture, as
Alexander Whyte, the nineteenth century Scottish Reformed preacher
directs:

> You open your New Testament . . . and by your imagination,
> that moment you are one of Christ's disciples on the spot, and
> are at His feet . . . with your imagination anointed with holy
> oil . . . at one time, you are the publican; at another time, you
> are the prodigal . . . at another time, you are Mary Magdalene;
> at another time, Peter in the porch.[8]

Neither the ancients nor our more recent forebears had resistance to
the idea of making their imagination into "sacred space" in service of
their faith. Long before New Age distortions, the imagination was a vital
part of spiritual formation. Since faith is the apprehension of unseen realities, imagination, when directed toward Christ, is one of faith's greatest
allies. When we "walk by faith, not by sight," we do it through the human

faculty of the imagination, envisioning what we know to be true by faith but that is invisible to the eye. In gospel meditation, unseen truths of the faith become experienced realities.

With my imagination I entered into the role of Zaccheus in Luke 19. In the quiet moments of meditation on this scripture, Jesus revealed to me the tree I had climbed to keep Him at a safe distance. It was the tree of service for Him. I heard Jesus say to me, "Howard, come down. I want to come home with you." As never before I experienced His desire to simply be with me. Knowing His desire for me incited my desire for Him. The result has changed the course of my life. An encounter with Jesus today is no less transforming than it was for Zaccheus.

Blaise Pascal's Holy Rationality

Seventeenth century theologian and mathematician Blaise Pascal possessed a faith based on experimental knowledge, the importance of which he learned in his scientific investigations. Truth was his passion, yet he understood the limits of the fallen mind when he confessed that the "heart has its reasons of which reason knows not."

Personal experience with Christ was at the heart of his faith. This experience came through meditation on the Gospels, as he explains:

> The figure used in the Gospel for the state of the soul that is sick is that of sick bodies. But, because one body cannot be sick enough to express it properly, there had to be more than one. Thus we find the deaf man, the dumb man, the blind man, the paralytic, dead Lazarus, the man possessed of a devil. All these put together are in the sick soul.[9]

As we enter the gospel stories we discover aspects of ourselves that need the touch of Christ as much as those sick bodies did: Lustful or vengeful thoughts are as contaminating as the leper's sores; prejudice is a form of blindness; fear of rejection or risk paralyzes the spirit; deafness to the cries of the hurting exposes deeper selfishness; the evil "spirits" of this culture tempt and, sometimes, "possess" me. Only the touch of Jesus directly and powerfully heals and transforms the soul.

CONSCIOUS OF NEW REALITIES

Brennan Manning's challenge in *The Signature of Jesus* summons us from complacency to conscious reality in our relationship with Christ:

> Philosopher William James said: "In some people religion exists as a dull habit, in others as an acute fever." Jesus did not endure the shame of the cross to hand on a dull habit. (If you don't have the fever, dear reader, a passion for God and His Christ, drop this book, fall on your knees, and beg for it; turn to the God you half-believe in and cry out for His baptism of fire.)[10]

Passion, the acute fever, comes from exposure to the reality of Christ. We come in contact with the reality of Jesus on the path of gospel meditation.

Again, as in praying the psalms, the methodology is quite simple. When we pray the psalms we allow our hearts to speak directly to God. In gospel meditation we allow the Lord to speak directly to our hearts. The approach that I have found most helpful is this:

1. Quiet yourself internally and externally.
2. Slowly read a passage from one of the gospels that you have selected beforehand.
3. Engage in the "application of the senses" discussed above.
4. Enter into the role of one of the characters in the passage.
5. Listen prayerfully for Jesus' words spoken directly to you. Feel His touch. Notice His actions.
6. Respond honestly to Jesus with thanks, praise, questions, or simply in quiet listening or loving adoration.

Obviously, this procedure suggests a flow rather than regimented steps. The essentials are simply to listen prayerfully to your living and present Teacher, the Holy Spirit of God, with an open and quiet heart. The entire process can be as brief as ten minutes, yet the results can be eternal.

The ongoing fruit of meditation on the gospel is highlighted by Dietrich Bonhoeffer:

The word of Scripture should never stop sounding in your
ears and working in you all day long, just like the words of
someone you love. And just as you do not analyze the words
of someone you love, but accept them as they are said to you,
accept the Word of Scripture and ponder it in your heart, as
Mary did. That is all. That is meditation. . . . Do not ask "How
shall I pass it on?" but "What does it say to me?" Then ponder this Word long in your heart until it has gone right into
you and taken possession of you.[11]

When this path has done its work, I do not simply possess the word
of Christ; rather, it takes possession of me. The reality of Jesus grips me
in the depths of my being. I experience the fulfillment in my life of the
apostle Paul's prayers:

- I pray that the eyes of your heart may be enlightened, so that
  you may know what is the hope of His calling, what are the
  riches of the glory of His inheritance in the saints, and what is
  the surpassing greatness of His power toward us who believe.
  (Ephesians 1:18-19)
- I bow my knees before the Father . . . that He would grant
  you, according to the riches of His glory, to be strengthened
  with power through His Spirit in the inner man; so that Christ
  may dwell in your hearts through faith; and that you, being
  rooted and grounded in love, may be able to comprehend with
  all the saints what is the breadth and length and height and
  depth, and to know the love of Christ which surpasses knowledge, that you may be filled up to all the fulness of God.
  (Ephesians 3:14-19)

In this direct experience with Christ through gospel meditation, we
feast on the Bread of Life and are "filled up to all the fullness of God."

And so we are moved out of disinterest in God into a new strength,
vitality, and passion for Him. We could not ask for any greater nourishment for our souls.

CHAPTER NINE

SILENCE AND SOLITUDE: THE PATH THROUGH SCATTERED LIVING

But Jesus often withdrew to lonely places and prayed.
LUKE 5:16, NIV

The quiet there, the rest, is beyond the reach of the world to disturb. It is how being saved sounds.
FREDERICK BUECHNER[1]

No assignment draws more puzzled looks and questions from my seminary students than the requirement to spend a half-day in silence and solitude.

Some see it as "wasting time" when they have so many "important" things to do. Others admit to some anxiety about the prospect of being alone without any diversions. Many wonder out loud, "What will I do for three hours?" And some are thankful that, finally, in the whirlwind of their lives they have an excuse to "Be still, and know that [God is] God" (Psalm 46:10, NIV).

When the students return from their foray into solitude, the reports are as varied as their initial reactions. Whether we embrace it with delight or resist it as an enemy, the radical change of pace is what evokes the strongest response. Most students, along with most of the general populace, have been intoxicated by busyness. Removing this ever-present stimulant causes a sort of withdrawal in the person. The dependence is so strong that it is no overstatement to call our "addiction to busyness" a predominant demon of our society.

BUSY DEMONS

Martha, the patron saint of busyness, typifies most of us in the western world. It was her busy preparations that removed her from the presence of Jesus. Luke describes her as "distracted" (Luke 10:40). I can think of no more accurate adjective for busy Christians. When I am busy I cannot help but be distracted, fragmented, disjointed. There is a difference between busyness and activity. I can be active and prayerful, but I cannot be busy and prayerful. They are mutually exclusive. And make no mistake, it is busyness that rules the day—and, all too often, our soul.

Busyness involves the pace of our lives. Long hours of hard work is nothing new to our time, but the frenetic pace of life today is a modern invention. More often than not in casual discourse the answer heard most frequently to the questions "How are you?" or "How's life?" is "Busy!" I am never quite sure whether I am supposed to be impressed by or sympathetic toward that response. For many, busyness conveys the illusion of importance and significance. The sacraments of this illusion are the ever-present cellular phones and pagers. Its holy book is the planning calendar. The irony is that the more we try to control our lives through these "time-saving devices," the more we lose our souls to the compulsions of efficiency and effectiveness.

Others, rather than feeling empowered by their busyness, feel victimized by it. One man I was meeting with complained of restlessness and distraction in prayer. I asked him, "What has your life been like lately?" He replied that it had been hurried, busy, and out of control. My observation to him was, "The person you are in work and life is the same person you are before God in prayer." Once we begin to live at this unhealthy pace, it is no longer within our power to slow down at will. The pace controls me rather than me controlling my pace. And, indeed, I do become the victim of my own busyness.

This busyness, a treadmill I have created for myself, is no longer a function of the number of tasks I have to accomplish, but a state of mind and a habit of the heart. Work has become the only acceptable addiction in our culture, especially if the work happens to be for God. We seem to subscribe to the philosophy of a bumper sticker I saw, "Jesus is Coming Soon. Look Busy!" Those of us in ministry, charged with the responsibility of spiritual leadership, are often the best candidates to serve as poster children for workaholism. We even turn praying into work as we enter prayer with our lists, guides, and books. Similarly, the forms of prayer currently catching the churches' attention, such as warfare prayer and intercession, seek observable results to justify the time spent. We feel the pressure to make prayer productive.

When this busyness invades our devotional times, we are guilty of what John of the Cross in the sixteenth century called "spiritual gluttony." Prayer and other spiritual pursuits are directed to my own fulfillment rather than to the worship and praise of God, or, as John puts it,

All their time is spent looking for satisfaction and spiritual consolation; they can never read enough books . . . They strive to procure [spiritual consolation] by their own efforts and tire and weary their heads and their faculties.[2]

The result is that there is no longer space for God in our busy minds and hearts. We find no rest for our weary souls. What path can we follow to escape this devouring "demon" and find the purposeful life we desire?

MAKING SPACE FOR GOD

A pioneer in matters of the soul, John of the Cross, I believe, speaks for all who need to conquer busyness. He discovered that one of the soul's most difficult tasks "consists in remaining silent before this great God." [3] *The Imitation of Christ,* Thomas à Kempis's masterpiece of devotion, has a section titled "On the Love of Silence and Solitude." The huge importance of silence and solitude for those who have sought first the kingdom of God throughout ages past is forcefully summarized by one astute theological writer.

If we read the biographies of the great and wise, be they states-men or priests, teachers or poets, Roman Catholics or Quakers, we shall find that they were men of long silences and deep pon-derings. Whatever of vision, of power, of genius, there was in their work was wrought in silence. And when we turn to the inner circle of the spiritual masters—the men and women, not necessarily gifted or distinguished, to whom God was "a living, bright reality" which supernaturalized their everyday life and transmuted their homeliest actions into sublime worship—we find that their roots struck deep into the soil of spiritual silence. Living in the world and rejoicing in human relationships, they yet kept a little cell in their hearts whither they might run to be alone with God.[4]

When we open up space for God in silence and solitude, we take the teeth out of the busyness that would chew us up. We begin to feel whole because we become centered in a humble and powerful aware-ness of God's presence moment by moment.

Silence and solitude together form a single path of quiet aloneness before God. They are the two sides of the coin of undistracted devotion. Though the two can be practiced separately, when employed together they place us before God in a very special way. We are open, receptive, and vulnerable to the Lord. All the outer props are removed. We are present to God, and He is present to us. You return from a time of retreat with one of two distinct feelings: the sense of having been on vacation or the sense of having been through a soul-cleansing furnace.

Jesus experienced both, and invites us to follow Him into silence and solitude.

A VACATION WITH GOD

Men and women most often use words like refueling, recovery, perspective, rest, and renewal to describe their times of silence and solitude. This reflects what our spiritual predecessors called *vacare Deo*—a vacation with God. A retreat into silence and solitude can be like a vacation for the soul, an intentional abstinence from the noise and crowds that typify our lives.

Jesus often sought these times of retreat (Luke 5:16) whether at night (Luke 6:12) or in the early morning (Mark 1:35). He invited the disciples to follow Him into this practice: "Come away by yourselves to a lonely place and rest a while" (Mark 6:31). Jesus issues the same invitation to our weary souls: an invitation to rest, recovery, and perspective.

Rest

One phenomenon reoccurs on virtually every retreat I have led: people sleep a lot. Many of us live in a perpetually tired state. Our bodies and souls are both in need of rest. When given the opportunity, such as a retreat, we sleep. Often there are guilt feelings around giving the body the rest it needs, but the soul cannot be alert when the body is fatigued. So sometimes the best thing I can do for my soul is to take a nap.

The soul also finds the rest it needs in silence and solitude. We enter the conscious awareness of God's presence by ceasing all activity, as Hallesby writes in his classic *Prayer*: "We can come into His presence and rest our weary souls in quiet contemplation of Him."[5] We discover the wonderful reality of simply being with our Lord. There is nothing to do, except to enjoy His loving presence. As far back as the second century, Christians realized the need for less doing and more being, as Ignatius, bishop of Antioch, wrote: "It is better to keep silence and to be, than to talk and not to be."[6]

Learning to "be" with Jesus in silence and solitude allows us to experience the promise of Isaiah 30:15: "In repentance and rest you shall be saved, in quietness and trust is your strength."

Recovery

Along with rest, our souls need to find recovery from the debilitating effects of the virus of busyness. Living a fractured, distracted, busy life leaves the soul in a sick, weakened condition. Just as the body takes time to recover from an infection that has afflicted it, so the soul needs times of silence and solitude for its recovery from the insane pace of modern life. The internalizing of the outward frenzy, however, is nothing new, as Gregory the Great comments: "The mind which is disordered by a rabble riot of thoughts suffers, as it were, from overpopulation."[7]

Recovery involves quelling the riot of thoughts in the mind and thinning the overpopulation of images and feelings that accumulate with an abundance of activity. Silence and solitude are the recovery room for the soul weakened by busyness.

Perspective

In the midst of being pulled in many directions by the demands of work, family, church, and a variety of personal interests, it is easy to lose perspective. The sheer volume of activity tends to level every task to an equal plane of importance. If interrupted by a child while completing the menial job of balancing the checkbook, we may impulsively respond, "Can't you see I'm busy?" We have lost perspective. We know that our children are more important than our checkbooks. We just don't always live that way. In silence and solitude we regain our perspective, or more importantly, God's perspective. Augustine described it as learning to "perform the rhythms of one's life without getting entangled in them."[8] Alone with God in prayerful quiet, the rhythms of life are untangled.

THE FURNACE OF CLEANSING AND TRANSFORMATION

The other side of silence and solitude is what theologian and spiritual guide Henri Nouwen has called "the furnace of transformation." I would only add that the transformation begins with cleansing my soul of the fluttering, distracting, unimportant things which cloud my vision so I wander misguided.

"In solitude," Nouwen writes in his book, *The Way of the Heart,* "I get rid of my scaffolding: no friends to talk with, no phone calls to make, no meetings to attend, no music to entertain, no books to distract, just me—naked, vulnerable, weak, sinful, deprived, broken—nothing. It is this nothingness I have to face in my solitude."[9]

The nothingness I faced in my first encounter with God in solitude was the bankruptcy of my own spiritual life. I was forced to see my egotism and idolatry. In solitude I was broken, humbled, and penitent. Then, in love and grace, God could begin to restore, heal, and transform me.

Silence and solitude also bring us face to face with the temptations of the world, the flesh, and the Devil. Our enemy is never more on the offensive than when we are on the cusp of making significant strides in our life with God. Often the entrance into solitude enjoins the battle with the Tempter himself.

As in all matters of the soul, Jesus is our teacher and guide. We witness His forty days alone in the wilderness being tempted by the Devil, emerging victorious in total compliance to the Father's will. These times of testing and conversion are necessary for us as well, if we are to be transformed into the image of the One who was tempted in all things as we are, yet without sin.

The fourth century "desert father," Anthony, retreated into solitude in response to Christ's call. For him it was a call to a life completely given over to prayer and solitude. In the silent, empty desert, Anthony struggled fiercely with the enemies of his soul. There the old self died and the new self in Christ was born. After a number of years he so possessed the spirit of Christ that thousands came out to the desert to see him and receive his counsel. On one occasion the seekers literally tore the doors off the abandoned fortress, where Anthony was in worshipful seclusion, in order to be with him. True Christlikeness, which is winsome and inviting, is developed as we patiently follow this path of silence and solitude.

My most recent pass through the furnace of transformation singed my pride in what I considered to be two areas of strength. I had always found comfort in times of disappointment in my faithfulness as a husband and father. I would tell myself that despite my many other weaknesses, in those two most important roles I had done well. That is, until on a half-day retreat, God graciously yet painfully showed me how I have failed my wife and children. I now have no trophies to point to in pride. I have come to the truth (I am a little slow) that every good gift issues from the grace of God. Now I realize that, in myself, I have no strengths, only weaknesses. But in Christ those weaknesses become vessels for God's power to be displayed. This lesson in humility was not learned through Scripture or study or fasting, but through solitude.

It does require faith in the goodness of God in order to submit to such deep interior work because we are never sure what might happen. It brings to mind the story in the Chronicles of Narnia where Lucy and Susan are discussing with the Beavers the prospect of meeting Aslan, the huge lion and Christ-figure. They ask if he is safe. Mrs. Beaver replies, "Course he isn't safe. But he's good."[10] Neither is God safe when I approach Him through silence and solitude — in that He is likely to shed light on things I have carefully tucked behind me in darkness. But He is good — in that He wants to free me from that destructive darkness I so strangely treasure. That fact gives me the courage to embrace whatever confronts me in the "furnace."

BENEFITS OF SILENCE AND SOLITUDE

All the benefits of walking the path of silence and solitude cluster around maturing in Christ. My experience and the experience of all others I have known or read about testifies to the necessity of the "hidden life" for spiritual formation to occur in the fullness that God intends. This was true for Jesus, for the disciples, the church fathers, the desert solitaries, and all the faithful who have followed in their steps through the present day. If I am serious about allowing Christ to be formed in me (see Galatians 4:19), then I will be serious about making silence and solitude a part of my life. The rewards are great. In addition to the time spent alone with God, which is reward in itself, I discover the gifts of listening, preparing, and surrendering.

Listening

Lord, teach me to listen. The times are noisy and my ears are
weary with the thousand raucous sounds which continuously

assault them. Give me the spirit of the boy Samuel when he said to Thee, "Speak, for thy servant heareth." Let me hear Thee speaking in my heart. Let me get used to the sound of Thy voice, that its tones may be familiar when the sounds of the earth die away and the only sound will be the music of Thy speaking voice. Amen.[11]

In silence and solitude this prayer of A.W. Tozer can become a reality in our lives. In the quiet of retreat, with all of the competing voices stilled, we learn to hear the gentle whisper of the Spirit of God. The first voice to be stilled is my own, as Howard Macy states with wit and wisdom: "To approach God with only an incessant stream of words is a filibuster, not prayer."[12] I need to heed the words of the prophet Habakkuk who said, "But the LORD is in his holy temple; let all the earth be silent before him" (Habakkuk 2:20, NIV).

This can take some time. On my first extended retreat it took me a day and a half to finally stop talking and start listening to God. When I did, I was able to hear the Lord.

In the classroom of silence I learn the ABCs of listening. Openness and receptivity are its necessary prerequisites. Listening is a skill that is developed with practice. There will be many times when I don't hear anything specific, only a settled sense of God's love or presence. The process is a gentle one and cannot be forced. The wise approach is to relax and allow listening to happen rather than trying so hard to make it happen. As we continue on the path of silence and solitude we notice one day what good listeners we have become.

Preparing

In reading Evelyn Underhill's book *Christian Mysticism*, I observed that for many of the great saints the contemplative life was previous to and preparatory for an active life of service. We have reversed the order. For us, if silence and solitude are employed at all, they are more often used as rehabilitation for those suffering from the stresses and strains of the active life they were ill-prepared to handle. We need to return to their earlier use as preparation so that, as Mother Teresa has learned, "The more we receive in silent prayer, the more we can give in our active life."[13] Whether lived out as a homemaker or third-world missionary, life is a spiritual conflict. We embrace God's kingdom of love and justice. We oppose the principalities and powers of darkness. Silence and solitude prepare us for battle.

Surrendering

To embark on the path of silence and solitude is, itself, a surrender of sorts. I let go of trying to control others through words by becoming quiet. I surrender the feeling of being indispensable by withdrawing from my active life. I give up my dependence on activity and noise that shields me from my own emptiness. I relinquish my self-protective knowing and doing in order to participate in authentic being with God. Finally, I surrender my unhealthy fear of God and place myself completely in His loving presence.

In silence and solitude many doubts, contradictions, fears, and anxieties may surface. I have often been asked what to do with all of these inner voices that seem to be vying for attention. Part of the gift of retreat is being able to honestly face these questions in God's presence. As I do, I surrender my need to settle every doubt, reconcile every contradiction, allay every fear, and calm every anxiety. I surrender the compulsion to "fix" the broken places of my life and leave those to a loving Lord. I no longer demand answers from God; rather, I learn to enjoy living the questions. In time and by God's grace, I trust that I will live into the mystery of life in a way that is more fulfilling than simply getting solutions to my problems.

In a word, in silence and solitude I learn to live by faith.

STEPS ALONG THIS PATH

I'm certain that for some, the possibility of silence and solitude seems a million miles away. How could it be possible for the stay-at-home mother of three preschoolers? Or for the computer programmer who has to work seventy-hour weeks to keep his job? It even seems difficult for those who have some degree of control over their own schedules.

But by beginning with a small, even if uncertain, step, anyone can walk the path of silence and solitude. As Nouwen has said, "Though we want to make all our time, time for God, we will never succeed if we do not reserve a minute, an hour, a morning, a day, a week, a month, or whatever period of time for God and Him alone."[14] In order to eventually develop a listening lifestyle, we must begin by setting aside a few moments to intentionally spend in quiet with our Lord. Here are some suggestions that incrementally build on one another:

1. Claim the "little solitudes" that already exist in your day.[15] The morning shower could symbolize a soul cleansing to prepare you to receive the day from God. Commuting could be God's gift to this culture as a ready-made, twice daily "sabbath," if we choose to embrace it by turning off the radio and listening to the softer voice of the Spirit. Nap time for the kids could provide a window of opportunity for a mini-retreat for the mom whose work never seems to be done. "Waiting time" at the store or at the traffic light can be turned into a reminder to "wait upon the Lord" in silence. At the end of the day, as you rest your head on the pillow, gently reflect on how God's presence was with you throughout the day.

2. Take a coffee break, lunch, or picnic with the intention of being quiet and alone with God. Rather than lunch with your coworker, slip off alone to the quiet solitude of a picnic in the park, even if the kids are along. Jesus did love the little children. Simply be aware of His presence with you, helping you serve the little ones.

3. Stay up a little later or get up a little earlier in order to find a few moments of solitude. Possibly a husband and wife could arrange to give each other "time off" to be alone with Christ in silence.

4. When possible, schedule your day more loosely. It can be wonderfully freeing to enjoy fifteen minute "spacers" between tasks or appointments. You can use this time to reconnect with God's presence in the midst of a busy day, as well as to gather yourself for the next meeting or task. I have found that I never miss those few minutes and that my awareness of God's presence is much greater.

5. Slow down. It is often the pace of life that pulls me away from the Lord. Walk slower. Drive slower. Eat slower. Notice. Pause. Listen. God is here. Slow down. When you do, you can carry a sanctuary of silence and solitude in your heart throughout the day.

6. Use times of physical exercise for silence and solitude. Enjoy the sounds of creation as you run or walk. Let the songs of the birds

remind you that you are of more value than the sparrows. Invite the Lord to run or walk with you and be conscious of His presence.

7. More intentionally, arrange to get away for a morning or day or even longer to a retreat center, park, or motel. Before you dismiss this idea, think of the many activities we go to great lengths to participate in that are far less significant than time alone with the Lord. Even if it means arranging childcare, losing some time at work, or missing the weekend sports event, is it not worth it?

God desires to communicate His love, grace, and peace to us, but sometimes we are moving too fast to receive them. In silence and solitude we extend the empty hands of faith to receive these gifts from Him.

A CAUTION

Linda had been looking forward to the day of prayer at the retreat center for two months. She couldn't wait to have some time for rest, quiet, and listening to the Lord. Life had been a bundle of worry, hurry, and flurry. She needed this time to slow down and be still. But when the day came and the silence descended on Linda, all she heard were voices of condemnation, whispers of past failures, and echoes of shame. If she opened the Bible she only saw reminders of her sins. Her day was ruined. She left more frazzled than when she came.

Linda needed to firmly quiet the voices of self-contempt. When some open-hearted believers such as Linda become quiet, all they hear are voices of condemnation. These are nearly always the result of some emotional wounding from the past. Scripture is clear: "There is therefore now no condemnation for those who are in Christ Jesus" (Romans 8:1). Sometimes we attribute self-contempt to the "conviction" of the Holy Spirit. However, every mention of the Holy Spirit's ministry of conviction in Scripture applies to unbelievers. When God wants to call the believer's attention to sin, it is done through loving, fatherly correction as described in Hebrews 12. It is Satan that is the "accuser of our brethren" (Revelation 12:10). God's voice is affirming, encouraging, and comforting. And that is the voice we listen for and respond to as we enter silence and solitude.

Many have found it helpful to enlist the support of a spiritual director to guide them during a time of retreat. This person could offer encouragement and guidance, as well as assist you in processing your retreat experiences.

In the following closing chapter, we will consider the many other benefits of having companions to walk with on these paths.

CHAPTER TEN

SPIRITUAL GUIDANCE: THE PATH THROUGH "LOSTNESS"

Two are better than one . . . for if either of them falls, the one will lift up his companion. But woe to the one who falls when there is not another to lift him up.

ECCLESIASTES 4:9-10

Behind every saint stands another saint. That is the great tradition. I have never learnt anything myself by my own old nose.

BARON FRIEDRICH VON HUGEL[1]

"Real men don't stop and ask for directions," decreed the refrigerator magnet given to me by my sister-in-law. This message recalled an event of years past that lives in both of our memories. I, the typical male, was willing to drive aimlessly for a seeming eternity without stopping to ask someone for directions to our destination. The magnet enshrines my stubborn independence. The result was simply wasted gasoline, but in the Christian walk the result is wasted spiritual energy. Yet for much of my Christian life, I have lived as though "Real Christians don't stop and ask for directions" was gospel truth.

Why is it that we are willing to go it alone on the spiritual journey in a day and age when we seek out personalized assistance in almost every other facet of our lives? We have accountants for our finances, stylists for our hair, medical specialists for virtually every part of our anatomy, travel agents for our vacations, therapists for our problems, attorneys for our conflicts, dentists for our teeth, and personal trainers for our bodies. Apparently, the only part of our life that does not warrant individualized attention is our relationship with God.

It took a major upheaval in my life to break my independence. Once broken, I was ready to ask for directions and ready to hear the Master's voice through His servants. Hopefully, you will not wait to seek guidance for your spiritual life until some sort of crisis makes you desperate for help. You can begin now to learn from the experiences of others how to walk along the path of spiritual guidance.

WHY WE WANDER ON OUR OWN

There seem to be two reasons that we have lost the godly spiritual guidance that generations of faithful Christians have treasured. James, in the fourth chapter of his letter, identifies both.

We Have Not Because We Ask Not

The first reason we wander on our own is a lack of awareness that guidance is available. Since we don't know where to ask, we don't ask. We identify with the lament of the psalmist, who cried, "No one cares for my soul" (Psalm 142:4). This cry is felt, if not heard, throughout the Christian community, as one study of congregational life demonstrates: There is no place in their structure and rhythm where a serious discussion concerning the state of one's soul is expected."[2]

Where are those whom C.S. Lewis described as the "particular people within the whole Church who have been specially trained and set aside to look after what concerns us as creatures who are going to live forever"?[3] We have lost touch with the sources of guidance for our lives in Christ that are centuries old and biblically deep.

We Ask But We Don't Receive

We live in a culture of incredible freedom. This is both a blessing and a burden. The blessings are obvious, but the burden is the responsibility of so many choices. Where should I live? What kind of work am I called to? Whom should I marry? Which schooling option do I choose for my children—public, private, or home? Which church do I join? These are all significant questions so, as Christians, we ask the Lord for guidance as they arise. But often we don't receive. Why? James says we are asking from wrong motives. When we only seek God's guidance at these times and not for the deeper issues of heart and holiness, then we reduce God's will to the mundane and the material. We want God's direction concerning the externals of life, while God's primary concern is not on the outward appearance but on the heart (1 Samuel 16:7).

By contrast, James calls us to humbly submit our entire lives to God, for God gives grace to the humble.

Several years ago I had the opportunity to participate with six other men in a four-day silent retreat. My agenda for the time was to "hear God's voice" in regard to whether I should move our family to a different city in order to be more effective in ministry. I was seeking guidance on an external matter. God, however, was more concerned with the condition of my heart toward Him. I had come to the place of being stagnant in my spiritual life. Perhaps "stuck" would be a better word. But I had no one in my life who was serving as a spiritual guide or pastor to help me out of those places. I was seeking guidance on the location of my house; I needed guidance on the location of my heart.

I have come to understand that the guidance of the Holy Spirit occurs on two levels of experience—interior and exterior. On my retreat experience I neglected the priority of the interior, the quality of my heart toward God, and focused on the less important exterior of the practical choices of life.

Giving undue attention to matters of God's will concerning external choices is one of the most common errors we make in our quest to live the Christian life. Since becoming aware of this in my own life, I have noticed it often in others who are seeking direction for their lives. An executive faced with the possibility of a transfer wanted my help in discerning God's will in the situation. In discussing his circumstances we discovered that he loved the world he was in and didn't want to give it up, regardless of what he thought God might want. It became clear that the real issue he needed to deal with, whether he moved or not, was his inordinate attachment to the comfort, security, and status of his current place. Once he did, he was free to make a wise decision regarding the transfer. When we are open to God's guidance concerning our heart toward Him we can have the absolute confidence that He is guiding us in the particulars of life.

GOD'S GUIDANCE

In recent years I have stumbled into three of these sources of guidance as I have sought direction in regard to how and where God was moving and working in my life. The general sense of God's guidance was nothing new to me, for I had experienced Jesus as my Good Shepherd guiding me to the right college, into Young Life, to Dallas Seminary, to my wife Janis, into ministry, and to various other locations. Because Jesus said that "my sheep hear my voice" (see John 10:27), I decided that listening intently was the proper response on my part. His guidance has come through three different "voices" that I have learned to pay attention to.

The Voice of Ancient Wisdom

The first voice I began to pay attention to in the process of seeking guidance was an echo from the past in the writings of John of the Cross. There was no specific "answer" here, but rather the igniting of a fire of passion to love Jesus. John recommended

Opening our innermost selves to the fire of God's presence:
We must allow Him access to the deepest places inside,
where our true will and desires dwell. It is there that He wants
to kindle us with the fervency of His love.[4]

Again, our Good Shepherd is constantly guiding our hearts into deeper intimacy with God, even as we seek direction in the practical issues of life. Christian psychologist Larry Crabb once remarked that if God wasn't answering our questions, we should look at the questions He is answering. These are the questions of the heart and of our relationship with Him. As Oswald Chambers has written, "God does not tell you what He is going to do, He reveals to you who He is."[5] I have found that when my heart is on fire for Christ, the practical decisions of life seem to come naturally.

Scripture

We hear the voice of the Holy Spirit in spiritual wisdom as we read Scripture and the classics of Christian spirituality. This is where we discover the questions that God is answering, which are eternally relevant. The primary text for this kind of reading is, of course, the Bible. When we read to hear the voice of God personally, the words of Scripture become to us, as we saw in an earlier chapter, spirit and life (John 6:63). This concept has traditionally been called *lectio divina,* or "spiritual reading."

Most of the reading we do is for information—gleaning a new insight, a helpful how-to, an interesting anecdote to share, or an inspirational thought to get us through the day. Scriptural truth is meant to be heard, not simply read. We "hear" the Word when we read slowly, reflectively, leisurely, repetitively, and prayerfully. When this happens the words become a tool to continue forming in us the image of Christ, rather than merely to inform us with facts about Christ. We allow the words not only to saturate our minds, but to penetrate our hearts.

Christian Classics

In addition to Scripture, many have found helpful guidance from the spiritual masters of past centuries. These Christian classics are excellent material for our spiritual reading because they speak of Christian experience from a radically different culture and context than our own. Their "blind spots" are different from our own, so they can challenge our images of God and our images of the Christian life that are culturally, rather than biblically, formed.

C.S. Lewis observed that we need the "old books" in order to correct "the characteristic mistakes of our own age" because "all contemporary writers share to some extent the contemporary outlook." The corrective is to keep "the clean sea breeze of the centuries blowing through our minds, and this can be done only by reading old books."[6]

Living in our materialistic culture, for instance, we may often assume that God's blessing on us is material—seen in terms of financial security, job stability, worldly success, and the absence of problems. Most of the classics, however, were written by men and women who knew little of worldly honor or material gain, but knew much of the peace of Christ in trouble, the sufficiency of grace in times of need, and the love of the Father in their hour of desperation. Therefore, their writings become an antidote for what poisons our spirit.

Where To Start

A few of the classics that have been the voice of ancient guidance for me are listed below with a brief description. You will no doubt find others that speak more clearly to you. But for now, these can be a start until you develop your own friends from the past.

THE IMITATION OF CHRIST
by Thomas à Kempis
(Look for the modern translation by William Creasy.)

For over 500 years, *The Imitation of Christ* has been the unchallenged devotional masterpiece for Christians. By most accounts it has become the most widely read religious book in history, outside of the Bible itself. In a simple yet profound manner, Thomas shows us the way of Christlike love and humility, and encourages us to follow and imitate. We desperately need to hear this ancient voice of humility crying out in our modern wilderness of inflated egos, self-importance, and unrestrained ambition.

THE CONFESSIONS by Augustine

Christians have two texts that must be taken with the utmost seriousness—the text of Scripture and the text of our lives. Augustine, better than anyone else and before anyone else, shows us how to see the hand of God writing the text of life and to pay attention to it.

THE PRACTICE OF THE PRESENCE OF GOD **by Brother Lawrence**
How does experiencing God's guidance become a habitual practice rather than an isolated event? This book leads us into the joyful practice of keeping company with God in the midst of all the details of ordinary life.

THE PURSUIT OF GOD **by A.W. Tozer**
Yes, there are twentieth century classics—but only a few! Because he is both American and from this century, Tozer knows us all too well. He goes for the jugular. Dismantling the self-centered and immature spirituality that is so rampant today, he replaces it with the authentic and mature pursuit of God.

An equally good place to begin for some may be one of the collections of excerpts taken from the classics such as Richard Foster's *Devotional Classics*, Bruce Shelley's *All the Saints Adore Thee*, or David Hazard's *Rekindling the Inner Fire* series of paraphrased classics.

The Voice of Contemporary Guidance

The second source of guidance emerged from a small group that I have been a part of for five years. One of the men had just returned from a trip to northern California where he had observed the many acres of vineyards immediately after the vines had been pruned. It struck him that the plants had not simply been trimmed, but radically cut back to the stalk. He compared that to the way God had been severely pruning his life.

His comment spoke directly to my situation. It helped me to see more clearly what God was doing and led me to reflect on what season of life I was in—pruning, dormancy, new growth, or fruitbearing. Again, there was no direct "answer," but there was direction which came from a voice of contemporary wisdom: another person's experience of Christ.

THE NEED

In the process of our working, playing, loving, and serving, there is a constant pull toward self-centeredness and away from God-centered living. Having a group of companions for the journey is a way of staying in the center of communion with Christ. As I considered changing jobs, through my fellowship group I realized that my reasons for wanting a change were self-centered rather than God-centered—more money, more security, more respect. I found Robert Bellah's insight both profound and true of me:

> We never get to the bottom of ourselves on our own. We discover who we are face-to-face and side-by-side with others in work, love, and learning.[7]

Neither rugged individualism, a lone ranger spirituality, nor a "me and Jesus" approach to life is an option for the Christian who seeks to be guided by God and to live biblically.

THE MODEL

In the New Testament, growing up into maturity and into the fullness of Christ occurs as the individual is part of a body or fellowship of other Christians (see Ephesians 4:10-16). The modern, small-group phenomenon has its roots in John Wesley's "class meetings" of the eighteenth century. These were groups of about twelve people who were "a company of men having the form and seeking the power of godliness, united in order to pray together, to receive the word of exhortation, and to watch over one another in love, that they may help each other to work out their salvation."[8] They were to inquire as to "how their souls prosper."

These groups were based on a healthy mixture of love, vulnerability, accountability, prayer, and Scripture, all directed toward a mature spirituality and unity in the body of Christ. Wesley's ideals can provide a model for us today of what a healthy small group needs to be: a setting in which each person will be able to hear the voice of the Holy Spirit through the contemporary wisdom of spiritual companions. As pastor and writer Alan Jones puts it, "God has so ordained things that we grow in the Spirit only through the frail instrumentality of one another."[9]

The Voice of Personalized Guidance

In the thick of my struggle to hear God's voice regarding my work situation I met with a "spiritual director," a man gifted and trained in the art of giving spiritual counsel. He asked me to consider prayerfully a few questions that pertained directly to my life and calling. This was the voice of guidance from God that was personalized to my experience, background, and present context.

Guidance in this form has been called spiritual direction, mentoring, soul friendship, or spiritual friendship. Definitions of spiritual direction are varied and numerous. I prefer the explanation given by spiritual directors Barry and Connolly:

> We define Christian spiritual direction, then, as help given by one Christian to another which enables that person to pay attention to God's personal communication to him or her, *to respond to this personally communicating God*, to grow in intimacy with this God, and to live out the consequences of the relationship. The focus of this type of spiritual direction is on experience, not ideas, and specifically on religious experience.[10]

ROOTED IN SCRIPTURE AND TRADITION

Spiritual direction has a long history both in Scripture and tradition. And this is significant because, as one writer put it, "Tradition is the democracy of the dead, extending a vote to our ancestors, refusing to submit to the small and arrogant oligarchy of those who are walking about."[11] The results are in, and spiritual direction has won a landslide victory when previous generations of Christians are allowed to vote.

Some biblical examples of spiritual direction relationships are Moses and Joshua, Elijah and Elisha, Jesus and Simon Peter, Barnabus and Paul, and Paul and Timothy. In the early church, the older women were instructed to encourage the younger in the practical matters of living out the faith (see Titus 2:3-4). The Pauline tradition of spiritual parentage reemerged in the desert mothers and fathers of the fourth and fifth centuries. Their firsthand experiences of God in solitude, their intense devotion, and their incredible gifts of discernment enabled them to offer others profound insights into the soul's development. This desert tradition continued in the monasteries of both the eastern and western churches. Ignatius, in the sixteenth century, developed a practical method of spiritual direction through his *Spiritual Exercises*, which became the most widely used tool for this ministry.

The reformers carried on the tradition in several ways that continue to this day. Spiritual guidance was offered one-to-one through personal letters of spiritual counsel penned by Martin Luther, Samuel Rutherford, John Wesley, and many others who followed them. Spiritual direction also took the form of house to house pastoral visitation, such as in the ministry of the seventeenth century English Puritan pastor Richard Baxter. Though his congregation was large, he visited each family annually, always taking notes in regard to the spiritual health of those in his care. As mentioned earlier in this chapter, John Wesley developed a form of group spiritual direction that focused on the question, "What is the state of your soul?"

WHAT DO I LOOK FOR IN A SPIRITUAL DIRECTOR?

We can receive this kind of guidance from our pastor, a Christian counselor, a godly mentor, a wise friend, or someone trained as a "spiritual director." Those who have been most helpful to me as spiritual guides have had some common qualities. Each director has been: (1) a person of prayer who prayed for me and with me; (2) someone who was able to see God's movements of grace in my life when I could not; (3) an individual who could accept me, just as I am; (4) a person strong enough to challenge me to go deeper with Christ; (5) a person of integrity, mature and passionate in his or her own relationship with Christ; (6) a good listener who could focus on the condition of my soul.

WHAT IS THIS RELATIONSHIP LIKE?

It is important to remember that the Holy Spirit is "your true voice," as the commercial slogan says, not any human guide. But the human guide can be the phone line that transmits the true voice of the Spirit. This kind of relationship functions best when marked by freedom, mutual respect, warmth, concern, humility, gentleness, and prayer. The value of hearing this voice of personalized guidance is due to the fact that "there are no dittos among souls," as the great spiritual director von Hugel observed. Each one of us is on a similar journey to Christlikeness, but it is not the same journey for all of us. That is why there are times when we will need a wise guide to point out the detours, identify the dead ends, and show us the smooth roads to travel on as we move along on our unique journey of dying to self and living in Christ.

A modern example of this kind of ministry is poignantly portrayed in the recent movie *Dead Man Walking*. Sister Helen is the spiritual advisor to a death-row inmate. She challenges him to take responsibility for his actions, confess his sin and guilt, and to receive forgiveness. She reminds him that Christ is present. She becomes for him the face of love, the face of Christ, as he walks through a literal valley of death. Through this relationship the inmate finds love, forgiveness, and is found by God. This is personal spiritual guidance at its best.

The Goal of Spiritual Guidance

Hearing these voices of guidance from our Good Shepherd steers us away from the kingdom of self and toward the Kingdom of God. The Word of God is contained in these voices and is "able to judge the thoughts and intentions of the heart" (Hebrews 4:12). The ultimate deceitfulness of our hearts (Jeremiah 17:9) requires that we pay attention to these voices if we are to mature in Christlikeness. The voice of ancient guidance delivers us from a culturally determined spirituality. The voice of contemporary guidance rescues us from a do-it-yourself spirituality. And the voice of personalized guidance saves us from a one-size-fits-all spirituality.

The fruit of receiving spiritual guidance, whether through a Christian classic, a small group, or a spiritual director, is beautifully described by Gwendolen Greene, who received individual spiritual direction from her uncle, Baron Friedrich von Hugel. She describes her experience:

> He preaches Jesus. And when he tells us of God his face is lit
> and illumined by some interior fire. He speaks like a prophet.
> He burns with his message — what he sees, he makes us
> see. . . . We are drawn into an awe and a worship of God we
> can never escape or forget.[12]

So, those of us who desire to live a life directed and focused toward God must heed these voices by stopping and asking for directions since . . .

- The revelation of GOD is whole and pulls our lives together.
- The signposts of GOD are clear and point out the right road.
- The life-maps of GOD are right, showing the way to joy.
- The directions of GOD are plain and easy on the eyes.

Psalm 19: 7-8 (MSG)

A BEGINNING, NEVER AN END

We have come a long way together, experiencing the art, practice, and paths that will "keep" your soul growing healthy in its journey to God. As we part company, what I want to say now is likely to seem odd as I have used terms like journey and path all through the writing. I have done so, as the Church fathers said, using an earthly likeness to convey an invisible reality.

But the truth is this: Our spiritual growth is not toward an end, but to a new beginning—to the One who is the Source of new beginnings, the Alpha, the Beginning of all beginnings. There will come a moment when He, in fact, will be making "all things new" (Revelation 21:5).

In light of this, I hope you will understand that this journey of spiritual growth is always an encounter with new beginnings. And some, in fact, experience a sense of growing freer, simpler, younger in spirit. (What else would we expect since we are becoming God's children?) And it is a path of fresh encounters with God's boundless forgiveness, fresh empowerments of grace—fresh "drinks" from soul-to-Soul meetings with Jesus, who is our living water.

The more we move and grow, in a sense, the newer we become, until that ultimate day when the Word is spoken and all things are, indeed, made new.

A WORD AFTER

By endurance you will possess your souls.
LUKE 21:19 (AUTHOR'S TRANSLATION)

The paths you have read about are only a few of the many that are available to you as your soul may need them. Origen, the third-century biblical scholar, wrote that the physician of our souls, namely Jesus, knows everything necessary for our spiritual health. Jesus is the doctor of our soul. He can diagnose the causes of our loss of soul. And He alone can prescribe the correct treatment to bring us back to health. In the Gospels we see Him making unique prescriptions to each individual. To Nicodemus it was, "You must be born again." To the woman caught in adultery, it was, "Neither do I condemn you, go and sin no more." To the rich young ruler, it was, "Sell all you have, give it to the poor . . . and follow me." And for each of us Jesus will lovingly diagnose the condition of our soul and apply just the treatment required.

So we need not feel overwhelmed by all the paths available for soul keeping. The only paths I follow are those that enable me to keep *my* soul. Each of us will have a unique combination of these paths based on the condition of our soul. Hopefully, as you have read and prayed about these paths, the Spirit has drawn you in a special way to two or three. Or possibly there is a strong desire in your heart for a particular path. I encourage you to listen to your heart and follow your desire. You may choose one path to address a deficiency in your relationship with God and another to deepen a strength. What we have in common is the life of prayer expressed in worship on the Lord's Day, in spontaneous conversation with the Lord throughout the day, and in the psalms. Beyond those essentials there will be much variety in our soul keeping. We are all on the same journey to union and communion with Christ, but we will travel different paths to reach our destination.

Soul keeping is not a sprint. It is a long-distance run. Endurance and faithfulness are essential. Shortcuts beckon. Detours hinder your progress. Potholes threaten. But no matter what, "Wait passionately for GOD, don't leave the path" (Psalm 37:34, MSG). At all times listen for the voice of the Lord "behind you, saying, 'This is the way, walk in it,' whenever you you turn to the right or to the left" (Isaiah 30:21).

If you follow these tried and true paths that will "keep" your soul, these words of Isaiah will become true for you:

> And the LORD will continually guide you, and satisfy your desire in scorched places, and give strength to your bones; and you will be like a watered garden, and like a spring of water whose waters do not fail. And those from among you will rebuild the ancient ruins; you will raise up the age-old foundations; and you will be called the repairer of the breach, the restorer of the streets in which to dwell. (Isaiah 58:11-12)

NOTES

Chapter 1
1. Thomas R. Kelly, *A Testament of Devotion* (New York: Harper & Row, 1941), p. 122.

Chapter 2
1. *Letters from Baron Friedrich von Hugel to a Niece*, ed. by Gwendolen Greene (London: J.M. Dent and Sons, Ltd., 1928), p. viii.
2. Robert Louis Stevenson, as quoted by Don Postema in *Space for God* (Grand Rapids, Michigan: CRC Publications, 1983), p. 26.
3. See C. Brown and G. Harder, "Soul," *Dictionary of New Testament Theology*, vol. 3, *Pri-Z* (Grand Rapids, MI: Zondervan, 1986), pp. 676-689.
4. Henri Nouwen, *The Way of the Heart* (New York, NY: Seabury Press, 1981), p. 9.
5. Greene, p. xxix.
6. A.W. Tozer, *The Pursuit of God* (Camp Hill, PA: Christian Publications, 1982), p. 11.

Chapter 3
1. Thomas Moore, *Care of the Soul* (New York, NY: Harper Collins Publishers, 1992), p. xi.
2. Quoted in Robert L. Wise, *Quest for the Soul* (Nashville, TN: Thomas Nelson Publishers, 1996), p. 29.
3. Charles Dickens, as quoted by Eugene Peterson in *Long Obedience in the Same Direction* (Downers Grove, IL: InterVarsity Press, 1980), p. 190.
4. Bruce Waltke, "Evangelical Spirituality: A Biblical Scholar's Perspective," *Journal of the Evangelical Theological Society,* vol. 31:1, March 1988, p. 16.
5. Leonard Bernstein, as quoted by Wise, p. 219.
6. Eugene Peterson, *Answering God* (San Francisco, CA: Harper & Row, 1989), p. 23.
7. C.S. Lewis, *The Silver Chair* (New York, NY: Macmillan, 1953), p. 17.
8. Samuel Rutherford, *Letters of Samuel Rutherford* (London: Banner of Truth Trust, 1973), p. 56.

Chapter 4
1. Kieran Kavanaugh and Otilio Rodriguez (tr.), *The Collected Works of St. Teresa of Avila*, vol. 2.
2. A.W. Tozer, *The Pursuit of God* (Camp Hill, PA: Christian Publications, Inc., 1982), p. 16.
3. C.S. Lewis, *Prince Caspian* (New York, NY: Macmillan Publishing Co., 1951), p. 136.

4. Bernard of Clairvaux, *Collected Works*, tr. by G.R. Evans (New York, NY: Paulist Press, 1987), p. 102.
5. Dante Aligheri as quoted by Gerald O'Collins in *Second Journey* (Herefordshire: Gracewing, 1995), p. 27.
6. David Fleming, *The Spiritual Exercises of St. Ignatius: A Literal Translation and A Contemporary Reading* (St. Louis: The Institute of Jesuit Sources, 1978), pp. 203-211.

Chapter 5

1. Robert Capon, *Parables of Grace* (Grand Rapids, MI: Eerdmans Co., 1988), p. 144.
2. Frederick Buechner, *Wishful Thinking* (New York, NY: Harper & Row, 1973), p. 34.
3. A.W. Tozer, *The Pursuit of God* (Camp Hill, PA: Christian Publications, 1982), p. 42.
4. *Augustine Day by Day*, ed. by John E. Rotelle (New York, NY: Catholic Book Publishing Co., 1986), p. 164.
5. John Chrysostom, as quoted by Paul Halsell in *Internet Medieval Source Book* (wwwfordham.edu/halsal/source/chrysostom easter.html).
6. Fyodor Dostoyevsky, *Crime and Punishment*, tr. by Constance Garnett (New York: Random House Inc., 1950), p. 322.
7. Capon, p. 182.
8. See Horst Balz and Gerhard Schneider, eds., *Exegetical Dictionary of the New Testament,* vol. 2 (Grand Rapids, MI: William B. Eerdmans 1991), p. 415.
9. Brennan Manning, *The Ragamuffin Gospel* (Portland, OR: Multnomah, 1990), p. 143.

Chapter 6

1. Thomas à Kempis, *The Imitation of Christ*, tr. by William C. Creasy (Notre Dame, IN: Ave Maria Press, 1989), p. 33.
2. Frank N. Magill and Ian P. McGreal, eds., *Christian Spirituality* (San Francisco, CA: Harper & Row, 1988), p. 145.
3. Magill and McGreal, p. 145.
4. Brother Ugolino di Monte Santa Maria, *The Little Flowers of St. Francis* (Garden City, NY: Doubleday & Co., 1958), pp. 58-60.
5. A.W. Tozer, *God Tells the Man Who Cares* (Harrisburg, PA: Christian Publications, Inc., 1970), p. 138.
6. Bernard of Clairvaux, *Selected Works*, tr. by G.R. Evans (New York, NY: Paulist Press, 1987), p. 142.
7. C.S. Lewis, *The Great Divorce* (New York, NY: The Macmillan Company, 1946), p. 72.
8. Karl Rahner, as quoted by Peter Kreeft in *Back to Virtue* (San Francisco, CA: Ignatius Press, 1992), p. 98.
9. Kreeft, p. 105.

10. Richard Foster, *Celebration of Discipline* (San Francisco, CA: Harper & Row, 1978), p. 115.
11. à Kempis, p. 65.

Chapter 7

1. Eugene Peterson, *Answering God* (San Francisco, CA: Harper & Row, 1989), p. 7.
2. J.L. Mays, *Psalms* (Louisville, KY: John Knox Press, 1994), p. 2.
3. Peterson, p. 117.
4. John Calvin, *Commentary on the Book of Psalms*, vol. I (Grand Rapids, MI: Eerdmans 1949), p. xxxvii.
5. Martin Luther, *Word and Sacrament I, Vol 35 of Luther's Works* (Philadelphia, PA: Fortress, 1960), pp. 255-256.
6. Peterson, p. 14.
7. C.S. Lewis, *Reflections on the Psalms* (New York, NY: Harcourt, Brace and World, Inc., 1958), p. 52.
8. See A.W. Tozer, *Pursuit of God* (Camp Hill, PA: Christian Publications, 1982), Chapters one, five, and six.
9. Hughes Oliphant Old, *Leading in Prayer* (Grand Rapids, MI: Eerdmans, 1995), p. 55.

Chapter 8

1. Oswald Chambers, *My Utmost for His Highest* (Burlington, Ontario: Welch Publishing Co., 1935), p. 55.
2. John of the Cross, as quoted by Ken Gire in *Between Heaven and Earth* (San Francisco, CA: Harper San Francisco, 1997), pp. 146-147.
3. A.W. Tozer, *The Pursuit of God* (Camp Hill, PA: Christian Publications, 1982), p. 46.
4. "Whereas *logos* can often designate the Christian proclamation as a whole in the NT, *rhema* usually relates to individual words and utterances." O. Betz in *The New Testament International Dictionary of New Testament Theology*, vol. 3, *Pri-Z* (Grand Rapids, MI: Zondervan, 1978), p. 1121.
5. Hans Urs von Balthasar, *Prayer* (San Francisco, CA: Ignatius Press, 1986), pp. 16-19.
6. Thomas à Kempis, *The Imitation of Christ*, tr. by William C. Creasy (Notre Dame, IN: Ave Maria Press, 1989), p. 30.
7. Francis de Sales, *Introduction to the Devout Life*, tr. by John K. Ryan (New York, NY: Doubleday, 1955), p. 84.
8. Alexander Whyte, *Lord, Teach Us To Pray* (New York, NY: Harper and Brothers, n.d.), p. 251.
9. Blaise Pascal, *Pensées*, tr. by A.J. Krailsheimer (London: The Penguin Group, 1966), p. 323.

10. Brennan Manning, *The Signature of Jesus* (Old Tappan, NJ: Revell, 1988), p. 70.
11. Dietrich Bonhoeffer, as quoted by Marjorie Thompson in *Soul Feast* (Louisville, KY: Westminster John Knox Press, 1995), p. 23.

Chapter 9

1. Frederick Buechner, *Whistling In the Dark* (San Francisco, CA: HarperSan Francisco, 1993), p. 108.
2. John of the Cross, *Selected Writings*, ed. by Kieran Kavanaugh (New York, NY: Paulist, 1987), p. 176.
3. John of the Cross as quoted by Louis Dupre and James A. Wiseman in *Light from Light* (Mahwah, NJ: Paulist, 1988), p. 292.
4. Brigid E. Herman, *Creative Prayer* (Cincinnati, OH: Forward Movement Publications, n.d.), p. 34.
5. O. Hallesby, *Prayer* (Minneapolis, MN: Augsburg, 1994), p. 149.
6. Ignatius of Antioch as quoted by Aelred Squire in *Asking the Fathers* (Westminster, MD: Christian Classics, Inc., 1993), p. 133.
7. Gregory the Great as quoted by Squire, p. 131.
8. Augustine of Hippo as quoted by Squire, p. 129.
9. Henri Nouwen, *The Way of the Heart* (New York, NY: The Seabury Press, 1981), p. 27.
10. C.S. Lewis, *The Lion, the Witch, and the Wardrobe* (New York, NY: Macmillan, 1950), p. 76.
11. A.W. Tozer, *The Pursuit of God* (Camp Hill, PA: Christian Publications, 1982), pp. 82-83.
12. Howard Macy, *Rhythms of the Inner Life* (Old Tappan, NJ: Revell, 1988), p. 51.
13. Mother Teresa, *A Simple Faith* (New York, NY: Random House, 1995), p. 7.
14. Henri Nouwen, *Reaching Out* (New York, NY: Bantam Doubleday Dell Publishing Group, Inc., 1975), p. 136.
15. Richard Foster, *Celebration of Discipline* (San Francisco, CA: Harper & Row, 1978), p. 93.

Chapter 10

1. Baron von Hugel as quoted by Jerome M. Neufelder and Mary C. Coelho, eds., in *Writings on Spiritual Direction By Great Christian Masters* (New York, NY: Seabury Press, 1982), p. 8.
2. Tilden Edwards, *Spiritual Friend* (New York, NY: Paulist, 1980), p. 100.
3. C.S. Lewis, *Mere Christianity* (New York, NY: Macmillan, 1960), p. 79.
4. David Hazard, ed., *You Set My Spirit Free: A 40-Day Journey with John of the Cross* (Minneapolis, MN: Bethany, 1994), p. 53.
5. Oswald Chambers, *My Utmost for His Highest* (Burlington, Ontario: Welch Publishing Co., 1935), p. 2.
6. C.S. Lewis, "On the Reading of Old Books," *God In the Dock* (Grand Rapids, MI: Eerdmans, 1970), pp. 201-202

7. Robert Bellah, *Habits of the Heart* (New York, NY: Winston-Seabury Press, 1982), p. 79.

8. Frank Whaling, ed., *John and Charles Wesley: Selected Writings and Hymns* (New York, NY: Paulist Press, 1981), pp. 35-36.

9. Alan Jones, *Exploring Spiritual Direction* (New York, NY: Winston-Seabury Press, 1982), p. 79.

10. William A. Barry and William J. Connolly, *The Practice of Spiritual Direction* (San Francisco, CA: Harper & Row, 1982), p. 8.

11. As quoted by Edwards, p. 35.

12. *Letters from Baron Friedrich von Hugel to a Niece*, ed. by Gwendolen Greene (London: J.M. Dent and Sons, Ltd., 1928), p. x.

AUTHOR

HOWARD BAKER is a spiritual director for Young Life (Rocky Mountain Region) and is an instructor in spiritual formation for Denver Seminary.

His current ministry includes seminary teaching, spiritual direction, writing, and leading retreats.

Howard resides in Littleton, Colorado, with his wife, Janis, and their children, Keely and Cody.

GENERAL EDITOR

DALLAS WILLARD is a professor in the school of philosophy at the University of Southern California in Los Angeles. He has been at USC since 1965, where he was director of the school of philosophy from 1982 to 1985. He has also taught at the University of Wisconsin (Madison), where he received his Ph.D. in 1964, and has held visiting appointments at UCLA (1969) and the University of Colorado (1984).

His philosophical publications are mainly in the areas of epistemology, the philosophy of mind and of logic, and on the philosophy of Edmund Husserl, including extensive translations of Husserl's early writings from German into English. His *Logic and the Objectivity of Knowledge*, a study on Husserl's early philosophy, appeared in 1984.

Dr. Willard also lectures and publishes in religion. *In Search of Guidance* was published in 1984 (second edition in 1993), and *The Spirit of the Disciplines* was released in 1988.

He is married to Jane Lakes Willard, a marriage and family counselor with offices in Van Nuys and Canoga Park, California. They have two children, John and Rebecca, and live in Chatsworth, California.

EDITOR

DAVID HAZARD is the editor of spiritual formation books for NavPress. He is also the editor of the classic devotional series, *Rekindling the Inner Fire*, and writes the monthly column, "Classic Christianity" for *Charisma* magazine.

For more than seventeen years, David has held various positions with Christian publishing houses, from editorial director to associate publisher. As a writer, he has contributed numerous internationally bestselling books to contemporary Christian publishing, some of which have been published in more than twenty languages worldwide. As an editor, David has developed more than two hundred books.

For the past twelve years, his special focus and study has been in the classic writings of Christianity, the formation of early Christian doctrine, and Christian spirituality.

If you liked SOUL KEEPING, be sure to check out these other books in the NavPress SPIRITUAL FORMATION LINE.

In His Image

Is it possible to be like Jesus in today's world? This book examines what it means to be like Christ, challenging readers to follow Him wholeheartedly and be transformed in the process.
Michael Wilkins

Love Your God with All Your Mind

Have you really thought about your faith? This book examines the role of reason in faith, helping believers use their intellect to further God's kingdom.
J.P. Moreland

Follow Me

Follow Me examines the kingdom of heaven, challenging readers to examine the kingdoms they set up—things like money, relationships, or power—that keep them from truly following Jesus.
Jan David Hettinga

The River Within

The River Within presents a vision of living life fully and passionately through the soul-freeing love of the Trinity. This new way of living will bring you closer to God as it plunges you into the joy of living.
Jim Imbach

The Glorious Pursuit

The Glorious Pursuit examines the virtues of Christ and how we can be transformed into His image by practicing them. We become transformed into Christ's image and are conformed to His will as we experience growth, maturity, and intimacy with God.
Gary Thomas

To get your copies, visit your local bookstore, call 1-800-366-7788, or log on to www.navpress.com. Ask for a FREE catalog of NavPress products. Offer BPA.

NAVPRESS ®

BRINGING TRUTH TO LIFE
w w w . n a v p r e s s . c o m